SNOBS' LAW
CRIMINALISING FOOTBALL FANS
IN AN AGE OF INTOLERANCE

STUART WAITON

Take a Liberty (Scotland)
6 Monifieth Road, Dundee, DD5 2RU
United Kingdom

First edition published 2012

Printed and bound by Scotprint, East Lothian, EH41 3ST.

ISBN 978-0-9571559-0-9 (paperback)

SNOBS' LAW
CRIMINALISING FOOTBALL FANS
IN AN AGE OF INTOLERANCE

TAKE A LIBERTY
SCOTLAND

Acknowledgements

This book developed from an initial petition to oppose the Offensive Behaviour at Football and Threatening Communication Bill. Thanks must go to the original ten individuals who signed this petition and to the 3,000 subsequent people who did likewise.

I am indebted to the supporters and fans representatives of various clubs in Scotland and in England who gave comments, support and criticism to the arguments made during the campaign against the Offensive Behaviour Bill.

Thanks goes to my friends in Take a Liberty (Scotland) who are a constant source of support and inspiration, and also to friends, family and supporters who helped to leaflet football fans and raise the profile of the campaign.

Acknowledgement goes to the variety of colleagues and associates who have helped with the ideas and development of *Snobs' Law*. To Donncha Marron and Ross Waiton in particular for the work they have done on this book, and to Kevin Rooney. A special thanks also goes to Alex Cameron for the design of the book itself.

Thanks must also go to the individual, or individuals, who invited me to the Scottish Parliament's Justice Committee to discuss the Offensive Behaviour Bill. Despite my criticisms of freedom and democracy in Scotland within this book there is thankfully still a great deal of scope for critical voices to be heard in this country. Whether or not this will continue to be the case is, in part, the subject of this book.

Contents

1

Introduction: The 'Game of Shame'

It is clear that the individual who persecutes a man, his brother, because he is not of the same opinion, is a monster.

VOLTAIRE, *THE PHILOSOPHICAL DICTIONARY*

IT'S A FUNNY OLD GAME. OR SO WE ARE TOLD. NEVER MORE SO PERHAPS THAN today when football is as likely to be found on the front pages of our newspapers as on the back of them. It's as if we have nothing else to talk about.

In Scotland in 2011, the strange obsession with football was illustrated by the various debates surrounding 'Scotland's Shame': Scotland's 'shame', for those of you who may not know, is sectarianism and in particular the sectarian behaviour of Old Firm football fans. In 2011 more newspaper articles were written about sectarianism and the Old Firm than had been written in any single year prior to this, and a significant new law – the Offensive Behaviour at Football and Communication Bill – was pushed through the Scottish parliament.

Football, as one wise old man noted, is a complete waste of time. In fact, it is the most beautiful waste of time yet invented by man. It's not only beautiful because of the game itself, but just as importantly because of the passion that the game brings out of generations of supporters. Being a football fan is more often than not an agonising experience; it is also an exhilarating activity, a place where grown men act like lunatics for 90 minutes, sing, shout, swear and scream at officials, players and opposition supporters. It is a walled-in space where for over a hundred years huge numbers of mainly men have gone and offended one another on a weekly basis. This makes it all the more peculiar that this new law passed in Scotland makes it illegal to be offensive at football. In many respects being offensive is football. But herein lies the problem – in a world that demands 'Respect' – football fans have increasingly come under the spotlight.

Tackling the offensiveness of football fans became the top priority for the Scottish government in 2011, so much so that they attempted to get the Offensive Behaviour Bill passed in a matter of weeks. This was an unprecedentedly short and anti-democratic length of time for such a piece of legislation. But who cares? They're only football fans.

Political interest in football is not peculiar to Alex Salmond, the Scottish first minister, or to the SNP government in Scotland – far from it. Football has become, for want of a better term, a political football. David Cameron, for example, perhaps following the lead of Alex Salmond, called his own 'summit' on football to discuss racism and homophobia in the game. We mustn't go back to the bad old days of 1980s racism, Cameron explained. The sequence of events that triggered this emergency summit, set up by the prime minister of Britain, related to a football player calling another player an insulting name and then the same player refusing to shake the offended player's hand when told to do so. The event was discussed in the context of racism, which transformed it into a national, and indeed an international issue, and yet for some this was a playground event, simply a form of name calling.

The Suarez-Evra affair followed weeks of news stories about a similar incident between John Terry and Anton Ferdinand. Suarez was banned for eight games for calling Evra a name, Terry on the other hand was officially charged by the police for a public order offence for doing the same to Ferdinand. He also lost the England captaincy despite not having been to court, and then came the resignation of the England manager Fabio Capello whose advice to keep Terry as captain was ignored. But more was still to come. We had a ban, a police charge, next we got a weeping apologetic young man from Swansea imprisoned for eight weeks for being racist about Patrice Muamba on Twitter.

In Scotland, similar events were unfolding, encouraged by the heated debate about the Offensive Behaviour Bill and the rhetorical outrage about sectarianism in Scotland. For Stephen Birrell, another online idiot, a few insulting words about Celtic fans was all it took for him to receive eight months in prison. This was before the new act had been passed.

Football and the behaviour of football players and fans was hardly out of the headlines in 2011 but this is not the first time that football has been something of a political football. In the 1980s, for example, there was a certain amount of concern, and some would argue hysteria, about 'football hooligans'. This concern about fans in the eighties is interesting and the initial chapter of this book starts here. However, there is a major difference between the concerns then and now. Then the focus of police attention was the actual violence of fans; today, in comparison, it is more likely to be name calling at football grounds that creates outrage and demands for action by 'right-thinking people'.

A generation ago football players 'telling tales' on one another for name calling, or fans being fined and arrested for singing offensive songs would have been unimaginable. Today it is becoming normal. Nevertheless, there is a genuine division in society over this issue, and one that could undermine the moral legitimacy of the law. For 'right thinking people' in both Scotland and England, imprisoning individuals for behaving in an incorrect fashion is understood and portrayed as the height of civilised behaviour. For many others, not only are the lengthy prison sentences being handed out seen as harsh, but the criminalising of offensiveness is seen as simply wrong. Here there appears to be an issue of some significance; an issue that has not been clearly debated in society: Should offensive words be made illegal? Is this part of a progressive fight against bigotry? Or are these developments authoritarian and infantilising – creating a situation where grown men are treated, and encouraged to act like children who tell tales on one another?

Much of the debate in Scotland about the proposed Offensive Behaviour Bill was posed in terms of how this new law would help to create a 'modern tolerant Scotland'. But can these developments be understood as having anything to do with tolerance, and what does tolerance mean today if it results in people being imprisoned for the things they say rather than the things they do? This is one of the key questions being addressed in this book. It is an issue that has historic significance in terms of our understanding of freedom and indeed with the understanding of democracy itself.

In England and Scotland football has become the centre point of the 'fight against bigotry'. In England this takes the form of kicking racism out of football; in Scotland it is both this, and the campaign to end sectarianism. Yet both campaigns come at a time when racism and sectarianism appears to be less of an issue in society than they have been for generations. Nevertheless, these campaigns, and the new laws to accompany them keep on coming. But why?

The strange case of 'Scotland's Shame'

In 2011, acting as though no other politician had come up with the idea of challenging sectarianism in Scottish football, the SNP government went on the warpath against bigotry in Scotland. Community Safety and Legal Affairs Minister Roseanna Cunningham, who has responsibility for tackling sectarianism, said: 'Racism, bigotry and sectarianism are not welcome in Scotland, it is totally unacceptable, and those who perpetuate this hatred will be punished through the full force of the law'. There was she argued, 'no place for bigots in a modern-day Scotland'. From now on Cunningham warned, 'anyone who peddles sectarian hatred – in any football stadium in Scotland, on the way to or from a game, or hiding behind a computer screen – could now face up to five years in jail'.[1]

The severity of the proposed law was justified on the basis that sectarianism was such a serious problem, or at least such a vile and unacceptable one, that tough measures were needed. The events of the 2011 season were also said to be 'unprecedented' and as such needed an 'unprecedented response'. The initial 'unprecedented' event was what came to be called the 'game of shame', a game between Rangers and Celtic that resulted in three red cards and a spat between Celtic's Neil Lennon and *Question of Sport* nice guy Ally McCoist. The result of this game was that Strathclyde Police and the first minister, Alex Salmond, called a football summit to tackle what was presented as a huge problem of sectarianism and sectarian violence surrounding Old Firm fixtures.

Talk of the 'parasite' that was sectarianism filled column inches for the next year as all sorts of social problems were connected to Rangers and Celtic fans, including domestic violence – an issue that had become something of a priority for the Scottish police. The proposed Offensive Behaviour Bill would tackle sectarian behaviour, and other forms of offensive behaviour at games in Scotland. It would also 'send out a message' to the country about what was and was not acceptable behaviour in society. As such, the Offensive Behaviour Bill aimed to; 'root out violent and bigoted attitudes and behaviour from Scottish society and make our communities safe'. If this did not happen, Salmond argued, sectarianism 'could kill Scottish football' (*Herald* 30th September 2011).

Not only the politicians but the police were also keen to highlight the problem of sectarianism in Scottish society and to illustrate their support for the proposed bill. Indeed, it was the Chief Constable of Strathclyde Police who proposed the initial Football Summit. Subsequently, the police have played a high-profile role in raising awareness about the various problems of street and domestic violence. Prior to the 'game of shame', for example, the Scottish Police Federation called for a ban on Old Firm games, saying they led to too much violence. The proactive nature of the police on this question helped elevate the issue of Old Firm violence prior to the start of the season, and prior to Old Firm games, helping to make a connection between Celtic and Rangers fans, sectarianism and also street and domestic violence. Indeed the extent of the police involvement in the battle against sectarianism was illustrated when they took it upon themselves to report Celtic to UEFA for 'illicit' chanting, an action that set a precedent in Scottish and possibly world football. Celtic fans had not suddenly developed a new offensive repertoire of songs, indeed you could make a strong case to suggest their songs are less offensive today than previously; what had changed was the intolerance of the police and the greater freedom they felt in defining and punishing offensive or 'illicit' singing.

The level of news coverage about 'sectarianism' and the 'Old Firm' was at an all time high in 2011 and, by November, resulted in such shocked headlines as, 'Religious hate crime hits four-year high' (*Scotsman* 19th November 2011). This was yet more proof, argued Roseanna Cunningham, of the shameful reality of religious hate crime in Scotland. What Cunningham failed to mention was that almost half of these 'religious hate crimes' were carried out against the police and only a fraction of them involved any violence. Nevertheless, various proposals were made to tackle this sectarian problem. These included: a new anti-sectarian police unit for football matches; new codes of conduct for players, coaches, officials and supporters; off-sales bans for Old Firm matches; new listening equipment for games to identify offensive songs being sung; and modern CCTV cameras carried by police officers to observe crowds and crowd behaviour. Many of these proposals have already been implemented, making football fans in Scotland one of, if not *the*, most scrutinised sections of society.

Opposition and issues
Initially, there was little opposition to the proposed Offensive Behaviour Bill. However, the attempt to rush the legislation through the Scottish Parliament raised concerns about the severe limitations this speedy passage would place on any proper scrutiny of the bill. Concerns were also raised by a few individuals within the press about the authoritarian nature of the legislation and controversy mounted about what could and could not be defined as 'offensive'; would 'crossing yourself in an aggressive manner', for example, or singing the national anthem be interpreted as a criminal offence?

Take a Liberty (Scotland) also campaigned against the proposed bill and eventually handed a petition with over 3,000 signatures to the Scottish Parliament. Importantly, fan groups at both Celtic and then Rangers also began to protest against the criminalisation of football fans, a concern prompted in part by the activities of the Scottish police, who appeared to be taking their lead from the politicians and ratcheting up their activities at games. Increasingly, stories emerged of fans being arrested for singing offensive songs. The use of existing laws was intensified, with more severe prison sentences being handed out to offensive fans. The most prominent amongst these being the afore mentioned Stephen Birrell.

The outrage surrounding this debate was exceptional. However, it is worth remembering that it was the 'game of shame', an actual game on the pitch rather than a battle in the stands, that triggered the initial Football Summit to look into new ways to police and regulate Old Firm violence. As Joyce MacMillan observed in the *Scotsman*, this was a 'game of shame' not because of fan violence, fan sectarianism or even fan offensiveness, but because of the actions of players and managers. Even the aggressiveness of the players was not particularly unusual for professional footballers and the spat between Neil Lennon and Ally McCoist was seen by many as little more than a case of handbags at three paces: Indeed the managers themselves appeared a little bemused by the furore after the game. Yet this was the 'game of shame' that prompted a football summit to 'do something about sectarianism'.

The speed with which the Football Summit was called suggests that the police and politicians were at the ready to target the issue of sectarianism in football. But what problems were they actually trying to resolve? Despite much talk about the problem of violence related to sectarianism and the Old Firm, it was noticeable that specific figures related to violence at games, or even on the street, were rarely used by either politicians or the police. The level of political and police energy given to the apparent problem of religiously-based violence is also curious given the fact that Scotland is an increasingly secular country. If there is religious violence in Scotland, it is likely to be declining rather than increasing if it is based in any way on the number of people who actually care about religion. Even the politically-charged nature of Rangers – Celtic games is far less significant now because the armed conflict in Northern Ireland has ended. Unless Scotland exists in its own bubble, and is bucking all modern trends, it would seem highly unlikely that there would be any increase in politically-motivated violence today. In fact, the reverse would appear to be far more likely.

Violence at games is less of a problem than in the past and is no more significant in Glasgow than in other major cities across the UK. This does not mean that this is 'acceptable', but the unexceptional level of violence at Rangers and Celtic games again raises the question of why the 'sectarian problem' has been so forcefully promoted. To some extent, violence is not the issue, at least in terms of the focus of the Offensive Behaviour Bill, which as its name suggests is more concerned about 'offensive behaviour'. Nevertheless, violence is often explicit and always implicit to the rhetoric surrounding the Old Firm and the 'fight against sectarianism'.

Much of the rhetoric surrounding 'Scotland's Shame' focuses on the issues of sectarianism and bigotry. Like racism, sectarianism is denounced as an evil in society that cannot be tolerated any longer. At first sight, this can appear entirely reasonable and the vast majority of people in Scotland would agree with this proposition. However, the very fact that the vast majority of people in Scotland wholeheartedly agree that sectarianism and bigotry are wrong, suggests that rather than sectarianism being an important issue to focus upon, it is actually of little significance to society. What does it mean when Roseanna Cunningham argues that, 'Racism, bigotry and sectarianism are not welcome in Scotland, it is totally unacceptable, and those who perpetuate this hatred will be punished through the full force of the law'? Should racism and bigotry be made illegal? Should we force bigots out of the country? Should we imprison people for expressing views that the majority of us find distasteful?

Hate is a bad thing and must be stamped out we are told. Or in other words, the government appears to be arguing that 'We hate HATE; so let's make it illegal'! But where does this leave the issue and ideal of tolerance that is promoted by Scottish politicians?

Much of the political argument about the 'sectarian problem' is couched in terms of what a 'modern Scotland' should be. But as we will see, this results in a fundamental irony: Opposing sectarianism may appear passionately tolerant and liberal, but it results in increasing levels of policing, new laws and increasing prison sentences. These new forms of regulation and punishment are often not related to the *actions* of individuals but their words, chants, songs and blogs. In other words, as the *Scotland on Sunday* noted, the debate about the Offensive Behaviour Bill 'mushroomed into a fundamental question about the ancient right of freedom of speech' (*Scotland on Sunday* 25th June 2011). What for many appeared, at first glance, to be an issue of violence and thuggery, turned out to be much more about basic liberties and the freedom of expression.

Another dimension of the Offensive Behaviour Bill worth noting is that it is self-consciously focused on football fans and football fans alone. It explicitly excludes artists and comedians, for example, from any legal recourse regarding their offensiveness. In this respect, perhaps what we are witnessing has a class dimension to it – less a progressive, liberal approach to life than the development of a prejudiced, anti-working class snobs' law.

It is also worth noting that all football fans are 'sectarian' in the sense of demonstrating a 'tribal' support for their team. The very point about many football fans' songs, chants and banners is to be 'offensive' to the opposition; to the opposition team, their fans and their traditions. In this respect, developing laws against offensiveness at football games could be seen as rather strange, to be missing the point and to be confusing football fan behaviour with wider political concerns: Indeed to be confusing problems in the real world with the pantomime of hate that occurs at games.

Finally, it is worth noting one curious irony about the Offensive Behaviour Bill (now Act). The talk about sectarianism, the focus on bigotry, the incidents leading up to the football summit and the launch of the bill all concerned acts of aggression targeted at Celtic players, individuals and the manager; yet the major impact of the new legislation will be to punish Celtic rather than Rangers supporters. Laws already exist to punish Rangers fans and others for singing, what are defined as, racist or sectarian songs. What the new act does is extend the reach of 'offensiveness' as a charge, making it something that could affect all football fans in Scotland and which will specifically 'even things up' in respect to the Old Firm. Although rarely expressed openly, a key impact of the act will be to target Celtic's Irish Republican chants. Alex Salmond made this point explicitly on BBC TV news on the 7th October 2011, when he explained that sectarian songs are not acceptable, and that 'IRA songs are not acceptable'.

One could argue that IRA chants are offensive, which they clearly are to some people. But it is difficult to argue that they are necessarily sectarian, at least in a religious sense. The final irony then, and another confusion about this whole issue, is that despite all the talk about bigotry and religious hate as problems to be addressed, one of the main impacts of the Offensive Behaviour Act is to criminalise songs that are political. The logic of what is being argued is that not only should bigoted songs be criminalised, but political songs that are deemed offensive should be made criminal. If we are to make political songs or ideas illegal, we need to ask what this tells us about our modern 'tolerant' Scotland.

Summary

This book is an examination of the way football fans are regulated. Developed initially around an attempt to understand the Offensive Behaviour at Football and Threatening Communication (Scotland) Bill, it begins by looking at the way fans were policed in the 1980s by the old conservative establishment who caged fans like animals and were ultimately responsible for the deaths at Hillsborough. This is done to contrast past forms of control with those being introduced by the 'cosmopolitan elite', a less overtly elitist, politically correct bunch, who are more preoccupied with controlling minds than bodies. Words, as John Terry, Luis Suarez and Stephen Birrell have found out, are treated today as though they are weapons, and the 'offensive' use of them can result in the loss of liberty.

Returning to the situation in Scotland, the question of 'sectarianism' is also explored. It is a term often used by the authorities to explain the violent nature of Old Firm fans and yet there is little violence amongst these fans especially at games and, as I will explain, there is little sectarianism either in any meaningful sense. By the end of the book I hope to convince the reader that the preoccupation with offensive football fans has little to do with the behaviour of fans themselves, and much more to do with the empty and intolerant nature of politicians and the authorities themselves. A range of concerns are raised here about the growing criminalisation of football fans, one being the rise of what I call the new sectarians. These are the new generation of fans who are being trained to be outraged at an ever growing list of words, terms and chants – an antisocial bunch whose fragile narcissism is encouraged by authorities who gain some sense of meaning by acting as their protectors. Watch out you linguistically incorrect riff-raff, your time is up because **_I'm offended_**.

2

Criminalising Football Fans: Hooliganism – the English Disease

The ideas of the ruling class are in every epoch the ruling ideas.

KARL MARX, *THE GERMANY IDEOLOGY*

DEFENDING THE OFFENSIVE BEHAVIOUR AT FOOTBALL BILL IN NOVEMBER 2011,
Community Safety Minister Roseanna Cunningham argued that, 'This bill will
not be the conclusive answer or the only solution, but it is the beginning of the
end' (*Herald* 19th November 2011). Chastising the opposition politicians who had
decided, somewhat belatedly, to oppose the bill, she proclaimed that:

> You can either do nothing and allow the status quo which allows the mindless bigot to thrive or we
> can take the strong action needed now and send out a message loud and clear that this behaviour
> is not going to be tolerated any longer.[2]

For anyone unfamiliar with Scottish politics, you could be forgiven for thinking
that never before had a courageous politician stood up and challenged football
fans and their bigoted behaviour. The reality is, in fact, the opposite. For over
a decade, Scottish politicians have dragged the 'sectarian bigot' out of the closet
time and again and kicked it around the park. Indeed, there were so many laws
against all sorts of offensive behaviour in football north of the border already
that it was difficult to know what new law Cunningham could possibly come
up with to tackle these 'mindless bigots'. If Roseanna Cunningham genuinely
believed that the 'status quo' meant doing nothing to control the behaviour of
fans she either knew nothing about the history of football regulation or had
never been to a game in her life.

However, Scotland is not alone in having a whole catalogue of laws to deal
with football fans. English policing and law in many respects has led the
way in fan regulations. Consequently, before looking at what is going on in
Scotland, we will first look at the case of the 'English Hooligan' and at the
changing nature of laws that developed in the 1980s and 1990s. The English
example is particularly useful because it illustrates major changes amongst the
authorities in their approach to regulating supporters, shifting from a more
overt and coercive line of attack against a perceived violent mob, to one where
'safety' became paramount, as did the management and control of not only
fan's actions but also their words.

Hillsborough

At a UK level, looking at the criminalisation of football fans, the Hillsborough
disaster is a case in point and a depressing example of how fans have in recent
decades been treated with contempt, caged in, and targeted as 'scum' by the
great and the good.

The FA Cup semi final between Liverpool and Nottingham Forest played at
Sheffield Wednesday's ground in 1989 resulted in the death of 96 people and
the injury of over 700 following a crush of fans who were unable to escape due
to perimeter fences that were familiar to grounds throughout England at the
time. Following this so called 'disaster' the *Sun*, notoriously, and to their cost,
lied about Liverpool fans robbing the dead and urinating on injured police
officers. This resulted in shops in Liverpool refusing to sell the paper, and to this

day many Liverpudlians still refuse to buy the *Sun*. The *Sun* had miscalculated, but in reality was simply pedalling the accepted conservative wisdom about 'scum football fans' that had been relentlessly reproduced throughout the eighties. The editorial of the 'respectable' *Times* newspaper, for example, had earlier in the decade discussed football as a 'slum sport played in slum stadiums watched by slum people' (*Independent on Sunday* 14th August 2011).

This elitist contempt for football fans was not specific to the 1980s. Indeed, ever since football developed as a mass spectator sport in the late nineteenth century, there have been snobbish outbursts about the sort of people who watch this 'slum sport'. The founder of the Scout movement Robert Baden-Powell, for example, moaned about the 'vicious game' watched by 'Thousands of boys and young men, pale, narrow-chested, hunched up, miserable specimens smoking endless cigarettes...hysterical as they groan and cheer in unison with their neighbours'.[3] Football stadiums themselves were designed and remained as dilapidated sheds for much of the twentieth century, usually containing a seated area along the side of the ground for the better off spectator, while the rest of the fans were allowed to huddle at either end of the pitch often without any protection from the elements.

Elitist contempt for football fans may not have been new, but for much of the post-war period it was rarely expressed openly, and was not a political issue of any significance. Through the seventies and eighties this changed, and an intense concern about the violent nature of football hooligans emerged as a problem to be addressed.

Old Snobs: Caging the mob

Violence at football grounds is not a new phenomenon. It's not that fans in the 'good old days' were constantly battering hell out of one another, but any serious study about trouble at games discovers that there have been occasional riots or pitch invasions at various times throughout the twentieth century. The interesting development in the 1970s and especially the 1980s is that suddenly occasional (and generally minor) violent disruptions at games became a major political and law and order issue. The term 'hooligan' began to be used, and attempts were made to understand football violence as a specific and dangerous thing in and of itself. Incidents that in the past may have been left to local authorities and police forces to deal with suddenly became national news, backed up with inflammatory political rhetoric, and as the eighties wore on, numerous new laws were developed for the first time that specifically targeted football fans. There was trouble at football games in the seventies and eighties, but to put things in perspective, as David Russell observed in *Football and the English*: 'In the early eighties, the arrest rate at football matches was at the very low level of slightly less than five per 10,000'.[4]

Different levels and types of confrontation at and around games may have occurred, and there were serious incidents, like the Heysel stadium disaster in 1985, where a wall collapsed on Juventus fans after a charge by Liverpool supporters resulting in the death of 39 people. However, neither this event, nor indeed other cases of fighting amongst fans, can fully explain the explosive and confrontational way the 'hooligan problem' was discussed and engaged with at this time. Rather, as a number of critical writers argued, extreme events and unexceptional incidents were interpreted and highlighted because of the wider concerns and preoccupations of the Conservative establishment at the time. In the 1970s, vandalism and violence of fans was redefined through both academic and governmental discussions about the problem. As Giulianotti explains in *Football Violence and Social Identity*, this specific social problem was now part of the governments' consciousness, and was an issue that began to be addressed in terms of social control measures.[5] As Greenfield and Osborn note, by the 1980s the regulation of football fans was 'based primarily upon a desire to control the public order problem of football hooliganism both at home and abroad'. A problem that the then prime minister Margaret Thatcher related to as a law and order issue, using legal and police powers to strictly control and regulate spectators.[6]

The first specific piece of legislation targeting fans that was introduced in the 1980s was the Sporting Events (Control of Alcohol) Act 1985. This act, which was similar to one introduced in Scotland in 1981, aimed to limit the alcohol consumption of fans, at and going to, games. This would be achieved in part by increasing the stop and search powers of the police, confiscating any alcohol found and encouraging the police to prevent anyone who was believed to be drunk from going to the match. Today, when drinking alcohol in many public places is illegal, this may seem of no significance, however this illiberal approach to the consumption of alcohol was unusual at the time. It was also an early example of the specific criminalisation of football fans in and of themselves. Here, football fans were targeted and treated as different and separate from the rest of the public. All fans were now seen as potential problems if they had a drink, and a relationship between football violence and all those fans who drank was established in law.

At the same time as football fans were being separated and labelled as different, they were also targeted as part of a wider group of 'deviants' in society, loosely known as the 'enemy within'. The recently released film, *The Iron Lady*, looking at the life of Margaret Thatcher who was prime minister in the 1980s, is a useful reminder about the confrontational nature of politics at this time. A time when mass strikes and militant trade unionism existed, when inner city riots by black people erupted that made the 2011 riots look like a tea party, and a time when the IRA were bombing not only the mainland, but were killing members of the British government. At a time of deep divisions within the country, conservatives targeted all these different groups and labelled them as violent deviants – what became known as the enemy within. Increasingly, an aggressive law and order approach was adopted to counter this 'enemy' and new laws were developed to increase the power of the police.

At the 1985 Conservative Party Conference, for example, the Home Secretary Douglas Hurd, after receiving a standing ovation for his praise of the aggressive policing of the riots, promised a new law to target trade union pickets and hooligans. Here, the trade union militant and the hooligan were presented as part of the same problem, with both being used to sully the name of the other: Trade unionists were hooligans, and hooligans were part of the leftist problem of violence, criminality and irresponsibility that was destabilising society.

The result was the Public Order Act 1986, an act that, as the name suggests, was focused on the issue of public disorder and the need to enforce order. In a variety of ways this act targeted groups of people, including football crowds and pickets, making it easier for the police to regulate and arrest people who were part of these 'mobs'. In contrast to much of the discussion about offensive behaviour in football today, especially related to the need to regulate words used by fans, the eighties concern with public order in football was primarily focused upon controlling the actions and movement of fans. Consequently, policing of fans was carried out by an intimidating mass of police officers. Supporters, especially away supporters, were at times treated as a virtual invading army, escorted to and from grounds by lines of officers and welcomed to the ground by riot vans, police dogs and mounted police. Football fans also became the guinea pigs for new forms of surveillance and crowd control mechanisms, with cctv and id cards first proposed as a way to regulate fans.

Within the Public Order Act provision was made for arresting people who used threatening, abusive or insulting words or who acted in a way or said things that could cause harassment, alarm or distress. However, unlike today, this understanding was based less on a concern about the harm done to individuals, than upon a concern to defend society's values, the peace of the Kingdom, British standards of behaviour and so on. It was a Conservative and moral use of the police and law to control the mob of pickets or the 'yob class' who went to the 'slum game played by louts in front of hooligans', as one Tory Lord described football and football fans at the time.[7] It was also part of a political, and at times, physical battle with the 'enemy within' who were criminalised and faced significant limitations on their freedom of movement – something that both pickets and football fans experienced.

The cages at Hillsborough, and the attitude and policing of crowds resulted in the 'disaster' in 1989 and the death of 96 people. There was no direct intent, of course, but the climate of contempt was well established amongst the authorities, a climate that encouraged police officers to view football fans through the aggressive regulatory framework of public order. Highly critical of this climate at the time, it was no surprise to me, as I watched the Hillsborough 'game of shame' in horror, to see the confused police officers forming a line across the pitch, with police dogs in hand, to prevent potential trouble, rather than helping the fans who were dying and desperately attempting to escape the crush.

Finally, when looking at the Public Order Act, one of the unexpected
outcomes noted by Andrew Ashworth was that the largest group of people who
used section five of the act and claimed to be harassed, alarmed or distressed
were police officers themselves. Ironically, but perhaps tellingly, the 'public'
– in terms of concerns about public order – turned out to be the police force
rather than ordinary people on the street.[8]

Standing up for England
Another way to start to look at the representation of football fans as a problem
in England is to look at the question of British or English nationalism.
In particular, the way in which English football hooligans were initially
represented as being un-British, and then became understood as far too British
– or at least far too English.

In 1987, the Plaid Cymru MP Dafydd Elis Thomas observed with some
frustration that, 'One of the singular achievements of Thatcherism has been
its capacity to enlist the rhetoric of British nationalism in its support'. He
was reminded of this, he said, during a debate about hooligans when the
suggestion was made by British MPs that, 'Belgian courts or Flemish jails were
unsuitable to judge or hold English football fans' (*Guardian* 21st December 1987).
For some good old British nationalists, hooligans may be scum bags, but they
were our scum bags, and Johnny Foreigner should take his hands off our boys.
This discussion was generated by the European ban on English clubs following
the Heysel Stadium disaster, an event and ban that led to a variety of concerns
about hooligans, many of which took a nationalistic form, but not always in
defence of 'our boys'.

As we have seen, the alternative – and more typical response of the authorities
to English football hooliganism – was to brand them as something akin to an
alien parasite on the otherwise wholesome British nation. Fans supporting
the English national team who broke the law while abroad, for example, were
often made an example of by the Conservative Party. Colin Moynihan the Tory
Sports Minister expressed his concern in 1989 that the Swedish authorities had
not charged any of the 102 English football fans detained after the World Cup
qualifying match in Stockholm. Prime Minister Margaret Thatcher, showing
her toughness against hooliganism, called on the FA to consider withdrawing
England from the World Cup in Italy the following year. A variety of arguments
and positions developed to explain, discuss or denounce the 'English hooligan
problem', but almost all of them centred around an understanding of the
importance of nationalism. Nationalism, as the Plaid Cymru MP recognised,
was a significant issue; a significant political force in the 1980s, and something
that most politicians across the political spectrum engaged with.

However, an interesting dimension of the Conservative's nationalistic
approach to politics and to hooliganism in general was the framework that
situated hooligans as part of the 'enemy within'. In 1985, Margaret Thatcher

went on the attack against Luton and Millwall fans for a violent incident the *Guardian* correspondent at the time described as nothing out of the ordinary. This, he believed, was her attempt to, 'lever football hooligans into place as the latest Thatcherite enemy within' (*Guardian* 26th March 1985). The point about the term the 'enemy within' is that it connected various 'deviant' groups in the UK with an external or foreign 'enemy', suggesting something profoundly un-British about the perpetrators of riots, pickets or violence in the stands. In other words, nationalistic ideas, ideals and rhetoric, were used to denounce hooligans and hooliganism (indeed the name 'Hooligan' is negatively associated with rowdy Irish immigrants): If one was 'proud to be British', one would look down one's nose at the riff-raff football hooligan. Jingoism and contempt for football 'trouble makers' were comfortable bed fellows. When patriotic England fans subsequently acted violently abroad they were defended by some against the bullying foreign police (unlike our friendly British Bobby), but denounced by many as yobs who were an embarrassment to the nation.

Nationalism was often used to denounce hooliganism and, ironically, was even used to attack the nationalistic English football fan.

A decade on and the type of nationalism promoted by the new elite had fundamentally changed, as had the way football 'hooligans' were policed and regulated. Under New Labour, who were first elected in 1997, not only was violence by English fans seen as a problem, but nationalism and jingoism in and of themselves became a growing concern – part of a whole new array of 'offensive behaviour' that needed to be policed.

Safety Police

Before looking at the rise of what the sociologist Anthony Giddens has described as 'cosmopolitan nationalism', and the way that the nationalism of English football fans became a cause for concern for the new elite, the issue of safety in football will be addressed.

Football dramatically changed in the 1990s. Most noticeably politicians suddenly and publically began to express their love of the beautiful game. Helped no doubt by the declining passion and engagement ordinary people had with politics, individuals like Tony Blair appeared to go out of their way to be photographed kicking a ball and shaking the hands of players of teams, in his case Newcastle, who they had apparently supported all their lives. (Rather foolishly Blair reminisced about sitting behind the goal watching Jackie Milburn, at St James' Park, a feat only possible if he did this when he was three years old and if he had taken his own seat to this all standing area).[9] This was a time when big money entered the game, the Premier League was set up, million pound players became the norm, police officers retreated and were replaced by safety officials, and all seater stadiums became mandatory. Safety became a major issue for clubs after the Taylor Report of 1990 which looked into the Hillsborough event. The report argued that there needed to be a 'higher priority given to the safety and well-being of spectators', with emphasis being placed on the comfort and safety of football fans.[10] The Football Licensing Authority and the new football safety officers became central to match day preparations. More widely, the question of safety grew tentacles and became a prism through which the game on and off the pitch was examined.

With the expansion of this culture of safety, the operational principle that emerged appeared to be predicated upon three assumptions: firstly that each individual needed to be kept safe; secondly, that other people should consequently be treated as possible sources of risk; and finally, that individuals were vulnerable and needed a greater level of protection than previously. Increasingly, the role of the authorities was to keep us safe. Safe not only from violent hooligans, but safe also from the person sitting next to us who may be drunk or smoking, and safe from the offensiveness of other fans.

Despite the less aggressive form of policing at games in the nineties, and a decline in the old elitist rhetoric targeted at 'slum people', legislation to control fans nevertheless continued and expanded. Following the Football Spectators Act of 1989 which proposed ID cards and passed what were to become Football Banning Orders (FBOS), the Football (Offences) Act 1991 was passed. This was a particularly tough law and order act which led to an increase in sentences for 'hooligans', set up the Football Intelligence Unit, made it a specific offence to throw an object onto the pitch, took a zero tolerance approach to anyone going onto the pitch and, most importantly in terms of how the policing of fans was to change, the act also criminalised racist or indecent chanting in a stadium.

In both acts, more than a hint of the old conservative focus upon football fans as a public order problem remained, but now the discussion began to shift towards a concern about safety. One way this discussion developed was around the notion of making football 'family friendly'. For David McArdle the criminalisation of indecency was understood to be nothing more than 'an attempt to sanitise the match day experience for the edification of a new breed of consumer'.[11] Still within the rubric of 'clamping down on slum people', these new laws began to stretch further out into areas of etiquette and language. Consequently, football fans once again became the guinea pigs of a new regulatory approach to public life, an approach that was increasingly legalistic but perhaps more importantly also worked through a new type of moralising about behaviour and offensiveness.

After Hillsborough, the image, perception and even self-perception of football fans began to change, as did the way fans were controlled and regulated. As Guilianotti noted, the 'post-Hillsborough period of May 1989... displays a steady withering of governmental 'law and order' resolve on football hooliganism'.[12] However, despite the reduction in some overtly aggressive, even brutal, forms of regulation and policing of fans, these new 'caring' forms of support and control went further and deeper, into areas of fan behaviour never touched before. If the 'hooligan problem' emerged as part of a collective public order question in the eighties, in the nineties problems with fans were framed more within an individuated climate within which private protection was encouraged and enforced. A kind of customer care approach rather than public order enforcement developed. Of course, the ideal football 'customer' was a particular type of person, someone acceptable to 'families' – to women and children – the assumption being that women and children do not like rowdy, crude, foul-mouthed men at football games. Towards the end of the century a new 'correct' fan culture was being encouraged, with the *Sunday Mirror* launching a campaign to, 'cut out the foul language which is driving families away from the game' (*Sunday Mirror* 3rd January 1999). This was based on a highly moralised perception of 'families' and was encouraged by the FA who launched a poster campaign instructing fans to, 'Keep the Passion, Lose the Language'.

Opposition to the more sanitised and commercialised form of football culture also developed at this time, with concerns about wealthy owners, price structures, the criminalisation of standing fans and a general concern about the way 'terrace culture' was being artificially manipulated and sapped of an 'authentic' fan culture. In *Moving the Goalposts*, Ed Horton argued that there was 'a policy of social cleansing, of making football suitable for the better-off by the simple means of removing the lower order from the stands'. In a similar vein, a Manchester United fan in *United We Stand*, complained of the 'antiseptic family values' and the 'deproletarianisation' of the game, while books of 'traditional' football chants were printed in an attempt to save the game from 'gentrification'.[13]

This romantic reaction to the 'gentrification' of football was, in part, a reaction to the growing regulation of fans. However, key aspects of these new regulations were either ignored or endorsed by these critics. Sociologist Carlton Brick, for example, interestingly observed that books like *You're Not Singing Anymore: A Riotous Celebration of Football Chants and the Culture that Spawned Them*, were often sanitised themselves and endorsed what was to become a new form of linguistic correctness. In *You're Not Singing Anymore*, the author explained his own censorship of certain unacceptable songs, explaining that:

> Many chants have been omitted [from the book] due to their racist or sectarian content. Some, such as the songs about the Munich Air Disaster that have been directed at Manchester United fans, are absent on grounds of common decency.[14]

In what appears to fit comfortably with the newly emerging official etiquette, those who were critical of the sanitisation of football appear to have not only accepted but to be promoting the same line as the authorities, one which includes the censoring out of offensive words and songs from the game.

As Brick argues:

> Here lies the greatest irony. Whilst formally oppositional to the new moralities of the football stadiums, the discourses of resistance are an implicit acceptance and appropriation of the new discourses of regulation that have been a feature of the policing and regulation of post-Hillsborough football fandom.

The former self proclaimed football hooligan Dougie Brimson, who set up the Football Party to stand up for 'real' fans, similarly argued that we need to seek, 'the removal of intimidation in all its forms, be it racial, verbal or physical'.[15]

For Brick, the unquestioning acceptance of this new 'caring' and 'correct' form of behaviour promoted in football was a problem, one that implicitly accepted a new form of regulation, control and even criminalisation of fans, for doing little more than singing unpleasant songs or behaving in an aggressive manner at games. Previously radical gender and race politics, Brick argues, under the auspices of the 'family friendly' game, were transformed into regulatory mechanisms for policing ever more aspects of fan behaviour.

New Cosmopolitan Snobs

In a previous section, above, *Standing up for England*, we looked at how nationalism was used to attack football fans, to label them as an embarrassment to the nation, or to equate them with the alien 'enemy within'. Part and parcel of holding 'decent' values at this time was to be British and proud. By the end of the nineties, with the rise of cosmopolitan nationalism, the world in many ways had turned on its head. The overt promotion of Britishness was now far more difficult and was as likely to be sneered at by key sections of the elite who would associate Great Britain with the barbarity of colonialism and imperialism. The Union Jack itself began to be seen as a potential problem – something to distance yourself from rather than wrap yourself in. Even British Airways, for example, got rid of the Union Jack emblem for some time and experimented with 'ethnic' tail fin decorations, as an alternative way to advertise themselves. Now to be 'decent', to be 'right thinking' meant rejecting jingoistic nationalism and embracing multiculturalism and anti-racism.

At this time a major focus of the hooligan anxiety was around the problem of the English fan. During the 1998 World Cup in France, when 100 fighting English supporters were arrested, there was shock and outrage, not just by old Conservatives, but by liberal and left leaning commentators. Despite the vast majority of fans having nothing to do with the violence a leading column in the *Guardian* argued that the England team should be forced to come home. 'What is it in the national character that brings on this mob violence', he asked, a national character apparently reflected in the words of one of the fans who shouted, "This is what the World Cup is all about" as he attacked some foreigners' (*Guardian* 16th June 1998). Being a nationalist, for this liberal commentator, was equated with being necessarily violent.

The Labour government had a love hate relationship with English fans at this time, wanting to praise them and hold them up as good people in an effort to promote England as the perfect place for the 2006 World Cup, while at the same time being highly suspicious of the jingoism associated with supporting the national team.

It was by now also entirely normal to work on the assumption that any problem within football could, and indeed should, lead to a national governmental response. Using laws to resolve perceived social problems became the norm under New Labour and a form of legislative diarrhoea emerged, resulting in the Labour government introduced the equivalent of one law for every single day they were in office. Demonstrating a pride in this new legalistic approach to social policy and the rising criminalisation of fans, the Football (Offences and Disorder) Act of 1999 was celebrated by the Labour Sports Minister Tony Banks as the, 'toughest anti-hooligan legislation of almost any country in the world'. It was quickly joined by the Football (Disorder) Act 2000. The result was that it became even easier to arrest and prosecute football fans, and to be even tougher on them in the courts. Consequently, stronger laws on ticket touts, stronger laws on racist and indecent chanting and also more far ranging Football Banning Orders (FBOS) were introduced.

Restriction orders were renamed 'international banning orders' and a key focus for FBOS was to target fans, especially England fans, who attempted to leave the country. Now an FBO could be given to an individual even if they had no prior convictions and the police were given the power to prevent a person leaving the country simply if they 'believed' there were grounds for a banning order. An FBO could be given to a person if they were violent, but violence was here defined (in the 2000 Act) as many things including threatening violence or using racist or abusive words. Consequently, a significant limitation on an individual's freedom regarding going to football matches or indeed travelling abroad was introduced, with the possibility of time in prison if the order was broken.

Interestingly, section 9 of the 1999 Act replaced section 3 of the Football (Offences) Act 1991 and now made it illegal for an *individual* to carry out racist or indecent chants. This appears to reflect a shift in how the problem of 'football hooliganism' was understood. Initially it had been made illegal to shout indecent or racist chants when in a *group*. The illegality was seen in terms of the 'mob' acting as an intimidating crowd and as such as part of a collective public order problem. However, through the 1999 legislation a lone individual could be arrested for the words he used, making it both easier to arrest someone, but arguably also reflecting the increasing importance being given to words themselves and the need to both protect people from these words and to punish anyone who uttered them. Rather than public order, the problem was understood as one of individual disorder: Of people who needed to be protected from offensive words and people who needed to be arrested for individual acts of offensiveness.

David McArdle notes that the police had rarely used the 1991 Act to arrest people for indecent or racist chants because of the difficulty of making arrests and getting convictions of this kind.[16] It is likely that these laws were also rarely used because the political priorities and pressures to use them were more limited. Under New Labour this changed and the police were pressurised to use the new laws. Now, courts had to actively explain why they did not use FBOs in football related cases, again putting pressure on the criminal justice system to increase the regulation of fans actions and words.

As the new millennium approached, culturally it was becoming less and less acceptable in England, and especially within the new elite, to wave the Union Jack and sing aggressive nationalistic songs. The new, preferred England fan would carry a St George's cross, or better still, ditch the flag and have it painted on their face while singing along to the official supporters' brass band that followed the team. If being nationalistic in the 1980s was for key sections of the British establishment normal, decent and even moral, by 2000 the new elite was more likely to see it, especially when carried out by working class football fans, as intolerant, offensive, potentially racist and even as a form of violence.

Racism the secular sin

Opposition and support for nationalism in football is not straightforward and both ambiguity and tension remains about supporting our national team and even 'our boys' when fans go abroad. However, as the 1990s progressed, the concern about overt nationalism, bigotry and especially racism escalated. Official anti-racism became an unquestioned moral absolute, and racism began to be treated as a new 'secular sin'. In many respects anti-racism became a mantra, and within football it became an unstoppable new mechanism for criminalising and regulating everyone connected with football; a new enforced etiquette.

As I write, there is barely time for the dust to settle on one national news story about racism in football before another kicks off. From Blatter to John Terry to Suarez and Muamba the racialisation of the discussions surrounding football appears to be increasing by the week. On *Match of the Day*, while discussing these issues, pundit Alan Hansen made the mistake of using the incorrect term 'coloured' to describe a black player resulting in the colour draining from the faces of his fellow presenters who realised his mistake. Discussing the issue of racism, Talk Sport's usually in-your-face presenter Adrian Durham noted, humbly and in acceptance, that he knew if he made just one 'slip of the tongue' on this issue he could expect to be washing dishes for the rest of his life.

For many anti-racists in the 1980s the fight against racism meant campaigning against deportations, fighting a political battle against racist immigration controls, or even a physical battle to stop violence against black and Asian families in inner city areas. By the end of the century and into the new millennium the 'battle' increasingly appeared to be with your own tongue, with words and 'offensiveness'. For critical race expert Christopher Kyriakides, there had been a metamorphosis in anti-racist activities, shifting away from a challenge of the authorities to become a form of policing used by the authorities.[17]

By the late 1990s anti-racism was becoming a key fixture of the safety, the regulation and the policing of games. In the appendix to David McArdle's *From Boot Money to Bosman*, he discusses the results of a questionnaire that he had sent to the 91 professional clubs in the English Football Association in 1997. The purpose of the questionnaire was to assess the extent to which these clubs had complied with the, 'Commission for Racial Equality's (CRE) request that they introduce three fundamental anti-racist strategies in support of the "Kick Racism Out of Football" campaign'. These requests were for clubs to: insert anti-racist messages in match day programmes; broadcast similar messages over public address systems; and carry perimeter advertising to show the clubs support for the Kick it Out's campaign. Although only 15% of the 65 clubs involved in the research had carried out all three requests, only 8% had not introduced any. On top of this it was noted that two clubs had additionally introduced dedicated 'hotlines' where fans could report incidents of alleged racial abuse (four other clubs were about to do the same). Twenty seven clubs said they had introduced other additional initiatives to discourage racially abusive behaviour. Only two clubs had done nothing at all.[18]

The Kick it Out campaign was launched in 1993 by the CRE and the Professional Footballers' Association (PFA) and, as McArdle notes, despite the fact that there had been other anti-racist campaigns at football, mainly launched by fans themselves, this was the first one to receive backing from the PFA, the Football Association and most of the clubs, illustrating the increasingly institutional nature of anti-racist campaigns. Interestingly, McArdle found that one club had initially refused to complete the questionnaire on the grounds that, 'the incidence of abusive behaviour towards the ethnic minorities is virtually non-existent...vigorously pursuing a policy...may be counter-productive by creating a problem that is not there'. Seven other clubs similarly argued that there was no record of racist incidents at their club or that they had found few problems even with away fans. Unfortunately, McArdle, like many previously critical sociologists and thinkers on the subject, appears to ignore the above comments and accepts without question that there was a problem of racism in football and to similarly be uncritical of aspects of the Kick it Out campaign. This is even more confusing when we look at the evidence received about the 'helpline' set up by one club. 'By the end of the season,' he notes, 'fans had used the hotline on between three and six occasions'. But was a 'helpline' that received between three and six phone calls illustrative of a genuine and serious problem of racism amongst football fans that could justify this and every other league club in England and Wales being encouraged to promote the campaign in their programmes, over their Tannoy system and on advertising boards around the ground?

This is not to argue that nobody at football was being racist; some individual clubs have had an association with far right groups and with racism. However, there appears to have been a remarkable acceptance both within football and even academia that, firstly, there is a serious problem to be addressed that necessitates football fans being told not to be racist and, secondly, that the Kick it Out and CRE campaign is an unquestionably good thing. This is particularly important as new forms of policing were and have subsequently been developed on the back of incorrect assumptions about a problem. In many other areas of life this over the top approach to a perceived social problem would be seen as something of a moral panic.

Anti-racist panic

In the 1970s sociologists began to talk of moral panics. These were panics by conservative sections of society that exaggerated problems not purposefully but because it fitted their prejudiced view of the world. For example, Stuart Hall and others wrote about the 'mugging' panic where the prejudices about British decline were dumped onto the shoulders of black inner city youth who were seen to be lacking in decent British values and increasingly becoming violent. Despite the reality of some crime taking place, critical sociologists questioned the law and order panic about black youth noting the exaggeration of the problem, the uncritical reporting of it, the political rhetoric surrounding the issue and the overt, aggressive forms of policing developed in response to it. Unfortunately, the same critical approach has not been applied to the rise of official anti-racism and the campaigns, laws and intense forms of police surveillance to stop football fans being racist.

One of the most interesting aspects of official anti-racist campaigns and debates about racism in football is that they have become more frequent at a time when racism in society is declining. As football writer Duleep Allirajah notes, 'At a time when terrace racism has virtually disappeared, the campaign to kick racism out of football is everywhere. Why?' No serious writer on the subject argues that racism in football has got worse in the last two decades, indeed many writers note the opposite is the case. In this respect the concerns raised by the clubs who argued that promoting anti-racism could be counter productive and did not relate to a genuine problem appear to have a point.[19]

As one football writer noted, the ironic thing is that when racism was commonplace on the terraces and when he was joining protests against Asian families being driven from their homes by racists or marching to the Trade Union Congress to protest against deportations, few people within politics or the media seemed to take any great notice of this.[20] Similarly, individuals like the footballer Pat Nevin stand out because they publically made an issue of racism towards black players in the 1980s and were ignored or told to keep quiet about it. This contrasts with today when speaking out against racism in football has become the done thing, a formalised performance enforced throughout the game.

Clubs in the nineties were asked by the CRE to take action to prevent the sale of racist literature outside their grounds. There was also concern raised about the BNP's influence over fans. But as Jon Garland and Michael Rowe note, extreme right wing groups' influence over fans has been 'negligible' and, 'previous observations that the far-right have enjoyed little success in the context of football remains valid'.[21] Following the script of anti-racism, the England supporters club re-launched itself. Now membership would be excluded to 'racists and xenophobes'. In the 2000-1 football season, new laws were passed to increasingly police racism in football and to promote anti-racism at games and yet there were only 17 arrests for race related incidents in the Premier League that year. This was a slight fall from 23 the previous season. This may well be one incident too many, but this is 17 arrests out of a total of 13 million people who went to watch these games, a problem of significance for 0.0001 percent of football fans.

The significance of anti-racism as an unquestioned new form of regulation and policing is problematic. As Allirajah observed in 2001, whenever new anti-hooligan measures are introduced, anti-racism is now the standard justification used.[22] To be a respectable Englishman you now had to be officially 'anti-racist' and to accept and even support the increasing use of CCTV surveillance and the tighter monitoring of fans in all grounds across the UK as part of the 'fight against racism'.

By 2012, the Equality and Human Rights Commission boasted that racial prejudice was now seen 'as a secular sin that is not to be tolerated'. Part of being British in the twenty first century, Mick Hume argues, is to be, and to be seen to be, anti-racist. For Hume, this official anti-racism is a new form of moralising. Ironically, it can be, and is, used to denounce foreigners, like the Spanish or East Europeans, who are seen as less anti-racist than we Brits. Of course, Hume notes, within Britain itself the new elite look upon the British white working class as the greatest sinners of all, a group who need to have the 'etiquette of official anti-racism drummed into them at every opportunity'.[23]

One of the important things about anti-racism today, Kyriakides argues, is that it now embodies the notion of 'unwitting' racism, a definition that emerged out of the Macpherson Report into the murder of Stephen Lawrence. This is a definition that lacks any relationship with politics, power or society, and transforms racism into an individual, psychological problem or one simply based on ignorance or a lack of awareness.[24] This almost mystical form of racism, where you can be a racist without knowing it, reduces racism to behaviour and language, and crucially – 'offensiveness'. If someone finds your words or actions racist and offensive – they will be recorded as being so, regardless of your intention. In many respects becoming an anti-racist was now akin to attending a finishing school, learning about how your unwitting use of words could be offensive, and being taught not to say the word 'coloured'. Consequently, those in authority, those with power – in the media, politics, and law – became the arbiters of this new etiquette.

Sadly, 'radicals' who once challenged the authorities over their demonisation and criminalisation of football fans are often the most authoritarian today. Garland and Rowe believe that anti-racism in football has not gone far enough and argue for the need to adopt more vociferously the Macpherson definition of racism. Using the example of Jason Lee – the footballer whose dreadlock hair cut led to the 'He's got a pineapple on his head' chant that was started by the comedians Frank Skinner and David Baddiel – Garland and Rowe argued that this was part of an elusive form of racism which pervades football and needed to be stamped out. As they argued, here we had a case of contemporary culture articulating, 'racialised themes in a coded manner that lacks overt racist language or references'. Remarkably, despite Skinner and Baddiel having no intention of being racist, and in fact being anti-racists, they became racist, as did fans singing the pineapple song, because Garland and Rowe decided this was the case. As Allirajah noted, 'In other words we are dealing here with a strain of racism so 'unwitting' that it is only discernible to trained sociologists'.[25]

Conclusion

The concerns about football fans had emerged in the 1970s and 1980s not simply because fans became more violent, but more importantly, the problem of hooligans was elevated as an issue by a conservative establishment battling with what they saw as an enemy within – a collective disruptive mob that was undermining good old fashioned British values and British society itself. Public disorder and the actions of the violent mob would be curtailed by the authorities getting tough and restricting the movements of various groups. At football, this resulted in a variety of heavy-handed measures being introduced, one being the creation of caged-in football fans. Hillsborough was the ultimate result of this.

By the turn of the century, football fans were still being heavily policed but now, through the language of safety and offensiveness, new forms of regulation emerged as the old established snobbery about 'slum people' intertwined with a new form of cosmopolitan elitism about the macho and racist nature of white working class fans. In many respects anti-racism replaced British jingoism as the default position for right thinking people. Ironically, anti-racism itself became very British. Into the new millennium the policing of racism in football increasingly became an accepted norm – a new moral good, and yet still the evidence of this problem did not exist, with only 44 arrests taking place this season across England and Wales for the 37 million people who attended games.[26]

Key to this shift was a move away from the concentration on policing the movement of the mob towards a regulation of individual's songs and chants. Initially, through the language of anti-racism, the policing of offensiveness emerged, opening the door to further demands that words be regulated and controlled in football grounds.

3

Criminalising Scottish Fans: Scotland the Offended

I disapprove of what you say, but I will defend to the death your right to say it.

EVELYN BEATRICE HALL, *THE FRIENDS OF VOLTAIRE*

IN SCOTLAND, AS IN ENGLAND, THE MOST SIGNIFICANT SHIFT IN THE POLICING OF
fans has been the targeting of offensiveness. The policing of violence amongst
football fans continues, and fans offensiveness is often directly or indirectly
associated with violence. But it is fans words rather than their deeds that have
increasingly become the focus of politicians and the police alike.

Here we look in detail at the Offensive Behaviour at Football and Threatening
Communication Act, and at the laws that preceded it. The purpose is, in part,
to illustrate how pointless this act actually is, because there are already so many
related laws in existence. The conclusion drawn from this is that the act itself
had little, if anything, to do with the need for new legislation, or indeed with
the problem of fans. It was almost entirely a self-serving political initiative
that played on old and new prejudices about football fans, and in particular
'sectarian football fans'. This will be discussed in more detail in Chapter 6 when
we look at the rise of the anti-sectarian industry.

The Offensive Behaviour at Football Act was passed at the end of 2011. Prior
to this a number of cases came to court, illustrating the existing powers held
by the police to prosecute fans for being offensive. For example, in October
2011 Rangers fan Jamie Hetherington was fined £1,000 and banned from
attending football matches for five years after openly singing a 'sectarian song'
that included the words, 'Fenian bastards'. As well as this, Hetherington,
a probationary police officer, was asked to resign from his post, the sheriff
noting that, 'You've ruined your career by your mistake. You brought shame
on your employers at Strathclyde Police'.[27]

If a 'mistake' could result in 23 year old Jamie Hetherington losing his job,
for one 17 year old Celtic fan it almost resulted in seven weeks in prison – again,
this was before the Offensive Behaviour Act came into existence. Having been
witnessed singing a 'sectarian' song, Michael (name changed) was visited at
seven o'clock in the morning by the police. He was charged, refused bail and
faced seven weeks inside while he waited for his trial. Thankfully, on this
occasion, the excessive nature of this treatment was reversed. Nevertheless,
the 17 year old spent five days in prison before his release (*Celtic Diary* 15th
November 2011).

Similarly, in May 2011, 19 year old Celtic fan Sean Smith was jailed for three
months because he made monkey gestures at Rangers player El Hadji Diouf.
Diouf was unaware of the incident that was reported to the police by fellow
Celtic fans who were offended by the gestures. After Smith's photograph
appeared in a Sunday newspaper, he was arrested and charged with a racially
aggravated breach of the peace. Sherriff Wood said that Smith had, 'brought
shame on the club you support and on Scottish football generally'.

Finally, and regarding the 'communication' aspect of the new act, the case
of Stephen Birrell illustrates the existing powers available for prosecuting the
words of fans. After writing offensive comments on a 'Neil Lennon Should
be Banned' Facebook page, Stephen Birrell was arrested. Sheriff Bill Totten

described Birrell's action as a hate crime not to be tolerated by 'right-thinking people of Glasgow or Scotland'. Totten added that he wanted to send 'a clear message to deter others' from writing things like, 'Proud to hate Fenian tattie farmers' and gave Birrell an eight-month prison sentence. Speaking after sentencing, Lesley Thomson QC, the Solicitor General, said: 'The Crown Office and Procurator Fiscal Service is absolutely determined to play its part in confronting the problems of sectarianism, religious offences and related disorder and violence'.[28]

Birrell's heavy sentence was influenced by his previous convictions. However, it was noted at the trial that there were no threats made or any incitement to violence in his Facebook message. Commenting upon the sentence, Alex Massie observed that this imprisonment for nothing more than writing unpleasant comments about people was a thought crime and a, 'shameful moment that demeans the country far more than anything said, sung or written at or about any damn football match'.[29]

Laws clearly already existed prior to the introduction of the Offensive Behaviour Act that could have been used to arrest and charge people for singing or writing 'offensive', 'sectarian' words. In the Birrell case in particular it was clear that the political climate against sectarian behaviour had encouraged a 'get tough' response from the criminal justice system that saw itself playing a key role in the battle against sectarianism. To what extent the criminal justice system should be taking on the role of sending us all 'messages' about sectarianism or offensiveness, or in spelling out what 'right thinking people' should think, is questionable. Either way, what was already clear and became increasingly clear with the Offensive Behaviour Act was that offensiveness in Scotland was becoming a criminal offence.

Laws, laws and more laws
The Offensive Behaviour at Football and Threatening Communication Bill was designed to tackle sectarianism and various forms of offensive behaviour at football games. It proposed making offensive behaviour that threatened public order a crime as well as making it a crime to write offensive or threatening comments on online blogs or social networking sites.

A common reaction to the bill, even by those who were generally supportive of legislation to tackle 'hate' issues, was one of surprise. In a number of submissions to the parliament's Justice Committee, the question was raised about the need for even more legislation to deal with offensive behaviour. The SNP government's aim was to push the bill through parliament in a matter of weeks, using emergency legislation procedures. This was something that was opposed by many groups including the Equalities and Human Rights Commission who argued for the necessity of a 'broader consultation process'.[30]

Listing some of the legislation that was already in place to deal with football and offensive behaviour, the Equalities Commission cited:

- Section 74 of the Criminal Justice (Scotland) Act 2003 which created the aggravated offence of motivation by 'religious prejudice'.
- Part 2, Chapter 1 of the Police, Public Order and Criminal Justice (Scotland) Act 2006 which introduced Football Banning Orders for a variety of offences, including stirring of hatred.
- Section 38 of the Criminal Justice and Licensing (Scotland) Act 2010 which created a new offence of threatening or abusive behaviour with a maximum sentence of five years in prison.

The Equalities Commission stated that given the above laws already in existence it was important that consultation was extended to ensure the new bill was necessary, lawful and proportionate.

In their submission to the justice commission, Dr Sarah Christie and Dr David McArdle went further still in questioning the need for a new bill. They noted that the five years for offensive behaviour in the new bill was already covered by the Licensing Act which could be used against threatening or abusive behaviour. Furthermore, common law 'breach of the peace' can again be used to similar effect. On top of this, other aggravated add-ons that inform sentencing also exist, for example:

- The Crime and Disorder Act 1998 covers 'racial' offences, section 74 of the Scottish Criminal Justice Act 2003 (mentioned above) covers 'religious' offences, and also the Offences (Aggravated by Prejudice) (Scotland) Act 2009 also covers prejudice related to disability, sexual orientation and transgender identity, which covers some of the categories in the proposed Offensive Behaviour Bill, with the other categories of colour, race, nationality and ethnic or national origin being covered in the 1998 Crime and Disorder Act. There is also the possibility of using section 50a of the Criminal Law (Consolidation) (Scotland) Act 1995 related to racially aggravated harassment and threats.

With respect to the threatening communication aspect of the proposed bill, Christie and McArdle note that section 38 of the Licensing Act already criminalises communication that a reasonable person would find threatening or abusive resulting in 'fear or alarm'. Otherwise, the common law charge of incitement could be used against such forms of communication.

Indeed, as the Stephen Birrell case proved, legislation was already in place for imprisoning anyone who wrote offensive (even non-threatening) comments on the web.

Christie and McArdle conclude their Justice Committee submission by stating that:

A commitment to addressing the sectarian behaviour is commendable, but hastily racing to pass legislation which does not go beyond what is already in existence is not. The only feasible justification for this measure is that it draws the attention of the media, the public and football's international authorities to the fact that something is being done to address 'Scotland's Shame'.

Forcing through new legislation with serious powers of imprisonment for the sake of some publicity is problematic in the extreme. Unfortunately, this did indeed appear to be a core aspect of the new bill's emergence and promotion by both Alex Salmond and Roseanna Cunningham. The new law was, however, also illustrative of the trend in politics to use ever more laws to resolve wider social problems.

Zero tolerance policing
The extent to which the above legislation has been used effectively appears to depend upon the actions, the priorities and indeed the experience of the police themselves. For example, a 'zero tolerance' attitude adopted and publically promoted by British Transport Police towards sectarian offences is likely to limit police discretion and result in more reporting by the public. In 2011 this resulted in newspaper headlines about how 'sectarian incidents reported on Scotland's trains…more than doubled this year amid a "zero tolerance" approach by police' (*Herald* 8th February 2012). It is worth noting that this 'doubling' was based on small numbers, the rise being 14 cases to 29.

Similarly, the use of FBOs has been internally promoted within the force and with sheriffs. By December 2010 there had been 101 FBOs issued. This relatively small number had increased significantly, partly because of 'efforts of the FBO authority and other stake holders to increase awareness of the FBO legislation'.[31] The small number of FBOs appears to reflect the sheriff's understandable use of them to target individuals who already had a history of violence. However, these numbers are likely to increase further and affect wider groups of fans with the creation of Football Liaison Prosecutors who will manage all criminal cases involving disruptive or aggressive fans (*Herald* 6th August 2011). In November 2011, Lyndsey Gray ACPOS (Association of Chief Police Officers in Scotland) FBO manager said, 'there's no question that numbers are going to rise' as sheriffs are encouraged to use them to increase safety at games (*Scotland on Sunday* 3rd November 2011).

A curious aspect of the new laws against football fans is that many of the 'crimes' regarding offensive behaviour come to light not because of the public reporting of them but because of specific police initiatives. Even more bizarre is the fact that many of these 'crimes' are actually committed against the police rather than members of the public. This is interesting considering a key aspect of this legislation relates to the apparent fear, alarm and harassment being felt by the *public*, or to the *public* order problem being created by the behaviour of fans. As we discussed earlier, in the case of religiously aggravated crimes in Scotland for example, the biggest group of people who 'suffered' religious abuse were not individuals or the community but the police themselves.

The more fan 'offences' and sectarianism is made into a political priority, the more the police go searching for 'sectarian behaviour'. This, of course, is not a one-way street, where the police are pushed along by politicians, as police chiefs have themselves been heavily involved in promoting anti-sectarian legislation and initiatives. For example, in August 2011 Celtic fan Michael Bailey was instructed to carry out 300 hours of community service after posting 'racist and sectarian comments on Facebook'. Bailey's 'crime' had gone unreported and appears not to have created fear, alarm, distress or public disorder amongst anyone in Scotland. But then, 'a police task force began reviewing internet sites after March's so-called Old Firm shame game' and discovered Bailey's comments and once again became the arbiters of offensiveness and self appointed defenders of 'right thinking people'.[32]

Police, politics, police

A key argument used by Roseanna Cunningham and other SNP politicians promoting the Offensive Behaviour Bill was that it was supported by the police. That the police are happy to receive more powers is perhaps not that surprising. More generally, it appeared that senior officers were particularly keen to be associated with the anti-sectarian tone of the bill. The repeated use of the idea that 'the police support this bill' illustrated that the government felt this was a winning argument. However some concern was raised about the extent to which the police/politician couplet was not entirely healthy. Concerns were occasionally raised, for example, about the extent to which the supposedly neutral Lord Advocate was happy to promote the bill.

Discussing this issue, the *Scottish Review* observed how Roseanna Cunningham had revealed that those police representatives consulted felt the new powers were welcome and overdue. However:

> Graeme Pearson, a former senior police officer and now a Labour MSP for the South of Scotland, pleaded in vain for caution. He asked where the evidence was that current laws were not working through failed prosecutions. He reminded colleagues that 'in most democratic societies, laws are enacted not as a result of the demands of the police or prosecutors but because communities identify the need for solutions'. He ended up in last Wednesday's debate asking fellow MSPs to recall the warning of Cicero, the Roman senator that 'the arrogance of officialdom should be tempered and controlled' (*Scottish Review* 21st December 2011).

Further concerns were raised about the Offensive Behaviour Bill and the role of the police in specifying what actually constituted 'offensive behaviour' when it was revealed that it would be individual officers who would make these decisions rather than politicians. In the discussion about the new bill, the government also refused to spell out which songs sung by fans would be illegal under the bill; this would again be left to the discretion of the police. As the government itself appears incapable of coming up with a definition of 'sectarianism', concerns about the flexibility of the law and the role of the police appear to be justified.

A further example of the role being played by the police in regulating the words spoken or sung by fans and acting as the arbiters of 'offensiveness' was clearly illustrated in November 2011. Following Celtic's Europa League match against Rennes, Strathclyde Police reported Celtic fans to UEFA for singing 'illicit' songs. The police action was not initiated by complaints from home or away fans, by Rennes officials, by members of the public watching the game on television or listening to it on the radio. There was no public order problem at this game, no related violence, no reported fear, alarm or harassment. Rather, the police took it upon themselves to decide what words were acceptable.

It is perhaps worth noting that, in many respects, the police simply don't like football crowds. This is understandable given the often volatile and hostile atmosphere in grounds of up to 50,000 people where officers scrutinising the crowds can receive a less than welcoming reception. Describing her first experience as a Special Constable at a football game, an ex-student of mine told me that it was chaotic: 'I felt as if the crowd was actually attacking me, it was a very strange psychological experience, we overreacted and arrested a 16 year old for throwing chewing gum'. Policing a crowd she noted was difficult, 'because you act in a defensive manner and don't think rationally'.

Things may be different for more experienced police officers. Nevertheless, the role of the police as promoters of policy regarding fan behaviour, as apparent 'victims' of verbal harassment and as arbiters of what being a 'right thinking person' means, is a worrying development.

Governing civility and hate
The increasing regulation of football fans can be situated within a wider development of laws and regulations in society. Looking back at the development of laws to regulate sectarianism in Scotland in 2006, the academic John Flint has noted that in exactly the same month that the then Scottish Executive published an *Action Plan on Tackling Sectarianism* in Scotland, the Respect Task Force in London published the *Respect Action Plan*. This plan was concerned with 'broadening and deepening' attempts to tackle anti-social behaviour in England and Wales.[33] Flint argues that:

> What these developments appear to represent is therefore a significant increase in the ambitions of government. The focus upon respect and tackling incivility and sectarianism are representative of what Frank Field has identified as a new 'politics of behaviour' in which regulating the conduct of citizens and their interactions in the public realm becomes an increasing priority for government.[34]

What this means is that the government and state in the twenty-first century is attempting to bring about 'cultural shifts' in the population and to reshape 'the habits of everyday life'. In the case of Scotland, a key aspect of this shift would be enforced by the police and courts in the increasing criminalisation of 'sectarian' and 'offensive' behaviour and the growing use of laws and policing to monitor and control 'hate'.

A significant and new framework within which this shift can be examined is that of 'hate crime'. These crimes are defined, as much as one can call it a definition, as crimes, 'motivated by malice and ill-will towards a social group. For example, a crime such as an assault that was motivated by someone's religion would be seen as a hate crime'.[35]

Traditionally, crimes that involved this type of malice were dealt with in common law by acknowledging the intent involved. A black man being beaten up for no other reason than the fact that he was black, for example, would be treated more seriously than a similar offence being carried out 'in the heat of the moment' following an argument. More recently, specific attention has focussed on 'hate' towards certain groups of people and provision made for longer prison sentences in such cases. The Public Order Act 1986 was the first to specify a crime of this nature with reference to race. From 1998 to the present (excluding the Offensive Behaviour Act) we have had a vast increase in these types of laws, with race, religion, sexual orientation, transgender identity and disability all made specific aggravated offences. As we noted in the previous chapter, the concern about offensiveness shifted from a policing of groups involved in racist chanting, to the criminalisation of an individual's offensive behaviour and, specifically, their offensive words.

Scotland set up its own Working Group on Hate Crime in 2004, and in 2010 the chief police officers organisation ACPOS published the *Hate Crime Guidance Manual*. As part of an attempt to encourage 'cultural shifts', the law, police and criminal justice system have become involved not only in crime-related matters but with behaviour more broadly. In the foreword to the ACPOS manual, Chief Constable Ian Latimer explained that, 'Contained within the ACPOS Equality & Diversity Strategy 2009-2012, "Celebrating and Valuing Difference", are four main commitments one of which is Hate Crime'.[36] Here, tackling hate crime is represented as part of the wider strategy of the police to celebrate and value difference. This can be seen as an attempt to change the culture of society (or at least the undesirable cultures within it), but also as a cultural shift within the police force itself – a force that had been seen by many, especially in the 1980s, as discriminatory. One particularly interesting thing about the ACPOS manual is its intensely therapeutic style, with regular reference being made to the impact of crime on the mental health of victims who apparently suffer post-traumatic stress, depression, and 'anger anxiety'. Through this therapeutic prism, specified groups of people are redefined, and arguably caricatured, as particularly vulnerable or damageable and therefore in need of extra protection from the police.

For anyone on the left of the political spectrum, and indeed within all mainstream parties today, tackling inequality is seen as a good thing. However, whether or not this can or should be the role of the police or laws is questionable. Discussing the rise of hate crime legislation in the United States, James Jacobs and Kimberly Potter note that, despite the intention of the radicals who pushed for these laws, it is not violent political extremists and racist organisations that have been affected by them. Rather, the vast majority of people being imprisoned for longer because of their apparent 'hate' are relatively poor, young, working class men who might shout something offensive during a drunken fight. Ironically, the colour-blind use of this law means that it is both white and black young men who are filling us prisons because of their use of incorrect words.[37] Jacobs and Potter believe that despite the intentions of these laws, they have helped to heighten rather than reduce a sense of racial difference in American society.

The above authors attempt to define what 'hate crime' actually is. There are all sorts of things people dislike or hate, they argue, but only some are defined by hate crime laws. In the end, they conclude that what we are really talking about is not simply hate but prejudice. In essence, they argue, people are being punished for their prejudices, or at least for saying things or shouting words that suggest they have prejudices.

In Scotland, the rise of laws to deal with hate and offensiveness have resulted in some worrying 'criminal' cases coming to light in recent years. In August 2011, for example, two girls aged 12 and 14 were investigated by the police for having used racist words on a social networking site (*Scotsman* 30th August 2011). Inspector David Mitchell, defending this use of police time, explained that 'writing something online is just the same as saying it in public'. But should it be a matter for the police and the law to punish twelve year old girls for saying things in public that are seen to be racist? In the same month, a sheriff was booed after finding a Palestine Solidarity Campaigner guilty of racist breach of the peace after he 'insulted' the Israeli flag of a college mate at St Andrew's University. The guilty man, Paul Donnachie was thrown out of the university for what many saw as a political, rather than racist, act.

More generally, regarding race and official anti-racism, the problematic use of offence procedures has been illustrated in the way that almost 2,000 Scottish school children have been reported to their education authorities for 'hate' related incidents. The majority of these incidents were carried out by primary school children, some involving children in nurseries; most being cases of name calling. As the *Scotsman* noted, 'Many of those accused of homophobia, racism and sectarian bigotry were merely toddlers'. Josie Appleton of the civil liberties group the Manifesto Club discussing this racialisation of childish name calling, argued that 'Children at nursery have just learned to speak so the idea that they can be racist is ridiculous'(*Scotsman* 4th July 2012).

Unfortunately this unthinking – zero tolerance – proceduralised attempt to govern the interactions, behaviour and words of people and even children in Scotland has resulted in the growing criminalisation and regulation of even the most trivial aspects of everyday life. It is also leading to serious problems within the criminal justice system itself.

Part of the rise of 'hate crime' policing appears to have been generated by a police attempt to re-legitimise themselves around more politically correct issues like racism, sectarianism and domestic violence. Discussing this increasing focus by the criminal justice system on certain types of offences with a court journalist, the point was made that many domestic disputes between neighbours in Scotland are now ending up in court specifically because they are said to involve racist or sectarian elements. This is despite the petty nature of many of the disputes and the scant evidence of any criminal activity. Concerned about this wasteful use of court time, a sheriff complained about 'racial and domestic abuse cases clogging up our courts'. Sheriff Douglas Cusine believes there is a massive backlog in the trials system which could see criminals walking free, in part, because of the backlog of race and domestic violence related cases that must be progressed by the prosecutor despite the lack of evidence that sometimes exists (*Scotsman* 8th November 2011).

Even police officers involved in the promotion of hate crime legislation and practices have raised concerns with myself about the lack of discretion allowed when dealing with these issues that involve offensive words. Once reported, the complaint cannot be withdrawn – even when the 'victim' of such an incident does not believe there was 'hate' involved, or when the culprit later apologises and the situation is resolved amicably. The zero tolerance aspect of the hate crime legislation means, as one officer noted, that they become 'unstoppable' once reported to the police.

The making of religiously aggravated offences

Finally, before we look at the Offensive Behaviour Bill in more detail, it is worth briefly noting how and why the Criminal Justice (Scotland) Act 2003 was itself introduced, an act that increased the sentences of individuals who committed an offence that could be shown to be aggravated by religious prejudice.

Following on from the legislation against racism, Liberal Democrat MSP Donald Gorrie proposed new laws in Scotland that would target sectarian hatred. Singing offensive songs at football games or on Orange or Republican marches was unacceptable in a civilised Scotland and something needed to be done, argued Gorrie. Donald Gorrie believed it was the role of government to not only establish what civilised values the public should adopt, but proposed that these values should be enforced through laws and policing.

As with a significant number of new laws developed in the UK in the last few decades, what was to become section 74 of the Criminal Justice (Scotland) Act 2003 emerged, in part, with the 'help' of an extreme case of violence, a case that was equated with the problem of 'sectarianism' in general, and one that was then associated with individuals singing 'offensive' songs. Through the 1990s, a worryingly reactionary trend developed in politics. Politicians, often despite warnings by themselves that 'there must not be a knee-jerk reaction' to extreme incidents, did just that and developed significant new laws and initiatives based on horrific one-off acts of violence. This was the case with: the death of James Bulger which resulted in a change to the legal age children could be prosecuted in court; the death of Victoria Climbie which led to the reorganisation of child protection services across England and Wales and eventually to the Every Child Matters document; and in the case of the Dunblane Massacre, a one off event carried out by a lone gunman, resulted in the emergence of rigorous vetting procedures covering millions of adults who have any contact with children. In the case of the 2003 Criminal Justice Act and the criminalising of religiously-aggravated offences, it was the brutal murder of Mark Scott that acted as a foundation upon which the law was built.

Mark Scott, who was 16-years old, was killed as he was walking home after a Celtic-Partick Thistle game in October 1995. The murderer, 23 year old Jason Campbell, had run out of a 'Rangers pub' as Scott passed by, slitting his throat and leaving him to die in the street. By the time Campbell turned himself in the following day, there had already been 50 phone calls to the police identifying him as the killer. This brutal murder was a pivotal moment. One key development was the subsequent setting up of the anti-sectarian charity *Nil by Mouth* in 1999 by Mark Scott's friend Cara Henderson. By the time the Criminal Justice Act was passed in 2003, there was cross party support for the act. Both Protestant and Catholic churches were keenly showing their support, as were both Celtic and Rangers football clubs. For all intents and purposes there was no opposition to the law.

The use of the Mark Scott murder to justify a new law targeting the singing of 'incorrect' songs is problematic in and of itself. It is even more problematic when one considers the peculiar, rather than typical nature of the murder. The killer was hardly a typical Scottish Protestant Rangers fan. In fact, his father and uncle were major Loyalist paramilitaries who had both received prison sentences for terrorist offences with the Ulster Volunteer Force. Unfortunately, what was a disgusting, extreme, incredibly rare event carried out by the nephew of the leading UVF terrorist in Scotland became equated with not only the question of sectarian violence, but with offensive words and songs sung by Celtic and particularly Rangers football fans. Nobody defended Campbell's actions; in fact, far from it, the response by local people in Glasgow and the wider Scottish public was one of utter disgust.

Nevertheless, sectarianism in Scotland increasingly became associated with violence, indeed with brutal violence and murder. But more than this, what until now had been seen as legitimate or at least non-criminal behaviour, like the singing of various offensive football songs, was suddenly to become a question of governance, something that a progressive Scotland could no longer accept. Discussing his 'hard line approach to sectarianism' and the importance of targeting songs sung at football matches and on Orange or Irish Republican marches in 2001, Donald Gorrie explained that:

They make violent people more violent and this has led to deaths after football matches. People can argue about how widespread it is but it is there as a cancer at the heart of Scotland which we need to tackle (Herald 5th March 2001).

For Gorrie, people can argue about how widespread it is, but who cares what the facts are: it's a cancer at the heart of Scotland. If this wasn't irrational and reactionary enough, this MSP asserts – again citing absolutely no evidence – that songs make people more violent and this leads to killings.

In summary, the brutal murder by Campbell and other forms of violence between fans was directly connected to the singing of religiously offensive songs: The songs or words are construed as part and parcel of the problem of violence and consequently something needs to be done to regulate and police it. Here, in a monkey-see monkey-do way, an elitist and contemptuous representation of people is given as a fact of life in Scotland. Songs equal violence – lock up the song singers! Ironically, the logic of Gorrie's approach, which treats grown adults like children or animals unable to control their violent impulses, means murderers like Campbell are given a ready-made excuse for their actions: 'It was the songs that made me do it M'Lord'.

Reality seems to have passed Mr Gorrie by. Tens of thousands of Rangers fans go to games, hundreds of thousands watch the games on television and many of them have sung religiously derogatory songs and yet they have not and do not slit the throats of a passing Celtic fans.

Following the trends of the time, a knee-jerk reaction resulted in a new law; this use of law itself being an ever-more important way that political questions like racism or sectarianism are addressed. With no opposition to the bill or to the accompanying rhetoric, a seamless and reactionary connection was made between football fans who sang offensive sectarian songs and the vile murder of Mark Scott. Unfortunately, this approach to the question of sectarianism became the building block upon which our 'modern, tolerant Scotland' has been built.

The 'Anti-Sectarian' Bill?

The Offensive Behaviour at Football and Threatening Communication (Scotland) Act was passed in December 2011 and came into force on the 19th January 2012. Two Hibs fans caught chanting offensive songs on a train were the first to receive fines under the act. Chief Superintendant Ellie Bird explained, with reference to what were described as 'racially derogatory' songs: 'These convictions and sentences send out a clear message that this sort of behaviour and criminality has no place in society' (*Scotsman* 14th March 2012).

The Offensive Behaviour Bill was promoted as one of the key new laws the SNP government would introduce following their landslide victory in Scotland. As we discussed previously, one of the interesting aspects of the bill was that it was promoted as a key weapon in the fight against sectarianism. The examples of sectarianism used as justification often referred to the targeting of individuals like Neil Lennon who were associated with Celtic Football Club. Yet a major feature of the bill was that it would 'balance things up' by targeting songs, associated with Celtic, 'that glorify the IRA'.

Up until this point, Celtic supporters could challenge charges by the police of religious aggravation if, for example, they were arrested for chanting 'Up the 'RA'. As the *Edinburgh Law Review* noted, before the Offensive Behaviour Bill became enacted, 'Reference to a political organisation (like the IRA), whatever its meaning in the Northern Irish context, could not by itself be seen in Scotland to amount to religious prejudice'.[38] Rangers fans, on the other hand, had no defence against the charge of religiously aggravated offences because of what were seen as sectarian songs about the 'Pope' and 'Fenian blood'. Similarly, in the case of the *Famine Song* – a relatively modern Rangers song, the lyrics of which are, 'Home, why don't you go home? The famine is over, why don't you go home?' – fans singing this have been legally defined as racist and charged accordingly. Lord Carloway argued that the song was racist because it 'calls on people native to Scotland to leave the country because of their racial origin'. The song is clearly offensive; in fact it is clearly intended to be offensive, as are many football songs sung about your nearest rival. But is it racist in the way Lord Carloway describes it? Was it intended as a racist song? As many Rangers supporters themselves are 'racially' Irish, this judgement is puzzling.

Consequently, under the existing legislation before the introduction of the Offensive Behaviour Act, Rangers fans could be 'done' for racist and sectarian-related offences, whereas Celtic songs had avoided both accusations, in law, if not in political rhetoric. This was despite attempts by politicians to 'clamp down on this sectarian behaviour'. What appears to have happened after Alex Salmond's initial grandstanding about the 'game of shame' was that this legalistic 'loop hole' became one of the few things that a new law could actually focus upon. Rangers fans' 'sectarianism' was already specifically being punished, whereas Celtic's was not. This aspect of the Offensive Behaviour Bill was rarely explicitly explained. However, on one occasion on BBC TV News, Salmond specifically said that sectarian songs are not acceptable, and that, 'IRA songs are not acceptable', as part of his justification for the new law. But what does this mean in terms of understanding the meaning of sectarianism?

We have seen how important both the police force and, specifically, chief police officers have been in supporting the bill. We have also seen how politicians have used police support as a strong justification for the new law. It is therefore interesting to note the ACPOS Football Sub Group submission to the Justice Committee which explains their desire to target 'political sectarianism' (i.e. IRA/UVF type chants) – something that was rarely if ever mentioned by politicians in their rhetorical promotion of the Offensive Behaviour Bill.

The ACPOS submission explains that, despite all the laws already in existence, 'there are still incidents which do not fit well with this statutory legislation'. They go on to raise reasonable concerns about the lack of a clear definition of sectarianism which they understand can take three forms: expressions of racial, religious and political opinion. Why racism is included in the discussion about sectarianism is not made clear. However, the interesting point here is the question raised about political sectarianism, something that ACPOS recognise, unlike race and religion, is not covered by existing laws. We need, they argue, 'to make a distinction between religious and political sectarianism', in part because, 'Section 74 of the Criminal Justice (Scotland) Act 2003 provides a statutory definition of religious prejudice, which is ill-suited to address the **political** sectarianism that is such a characteristic of Old Firm animosity'.

Here, the bold lettering used by the police chiefs, expresses well their frustration at the limited, religious way that sectarianism was being policed. As they note, with some justification, 'The Lord Advocate's guidance on 'prejudice relating to religion' does not address the issue of Irish Loyalist/ Republican **political** prejudice, which is arguably the greater driver of sectarian behaviour in Scotland'. By focusing on the political dimension to the Rangers/Celtic rivalry, the ACPOS submission inadvertently raises doubts about the usefulness of seeing a religious and perhaps especially a racial element within 'sectarian' football chants. Pro-IRA or UVF chants, they note, do not fit comfortably within the idea of protecting a 'social or cultural group'. Indeed they do not.

In essence, the police were dealing with the problem as they saw it. A key part of Celtic and Rangers chants and rivalry takes the form not of religious or racial difference but political difference. They both use chants specifically about 'terrorist' groups and these chants, as far as the police (indeed as far as Alex Salmond and other MSPs) are concerned, are offensive and should not be allowed.

The use of the idea of 'offensiveness' at football in the new bill can be seen, in part, as a way of criminalising the political songs and banners of both Rangers and Celtic supporters. Perhaps Celtic supporters are especially in mind here as they had, in theory at least, been able to sing 'Up the 'RA' and other 'offensive' Irish Republican songs without being criminalised. That this aspect of the bill was rarely highlighted during its transition through the Scottish Parliament is both interesting and worrying as it avoided a proper discussion about the potentially authoritarian aspects of criminalising political songs, chants and slogans.

From a purely 'offensive' point of view, the police chiefs had a point. Many people may find IRA or UVF chants *offensive*. But does this mean that what we are witnessing is, in essence, the criminalisation of offensiveness? If this is the case, it is again a worrying development in what is supposed to be a free society. In her closing remarks in parliament to the second stage discussion of the bill, Roseanna Cunningham used the example of Celtic Football Club being 'embarrassed' about their own fans chanting IRA songs. Closing remarks are usually the ones you hold back and use as the final hurrah, the final nail in the coffin: 'Now there can be no opposition to that' – the end. But since when did the state, police, judges and prison service, backed by the government, become a force for preventing 'embarrassment'?

The Offensive Behaviour Bill

When the bill was initially proposed there was a lot of confusion about the necessity of it, about the confused nature of it and about the short length of time being allowed to discuss the bill before it was to be voted upon. Legally speaking, the bill appeared to be all over the place, hastily drafted and largely unnecessary. One legal commentator described it as the worst piece of legislation he had ever seen. More outrage was expressed about the emergency legislation procedure being used by the government that left no time for serious discussion or scrutiny of the bill. For many, the majority SNP government was seen to be acting in an undemocratic manner.

One reason for the bill, as we have discussed, is the targeting of 'political sectarianism'. Another, which we will look at in more detail in a later chapter, is the political grandstanding taking place. Standing up and denouncing sectarianism is the moral equivalent of standing up anywhere in the UK and denouncing racism: It is an untouchable position and one that Scottish politicians have fallen back upon time and again in the last decade. This is no doubt one of the reasons why Alex Salmond thought he could get away with pushing the bill through parliament in a matter of weeks. Thankfully, the level of opposition to this time scale forced the government to extend the debate and to follow normal democratic standards.

The bill itself faced little opposition initially, with 103 MSPs voting in favour of the general principles of it and five voting against. However, as vocal opposition from fans, organizations such as *Take a Liberty (Scotland)* and commentators in the press increased, dissenting voices grew louder within parliament. Indeed, one of the contenders for the Scottish Labour Party leadership, Tom Harris, came to Ibrox to hand out *Take a Liberty (Scotland)* leaflets defending the right to be offensive at football matches.[39] By the time the bill was passed, by 64 votes to 57, the SNP were left isolated as the other major political parties voted against it. Nevertheless, with the SNP majority in parliament, the bill was enacted.

The Offensive Behaviour at Football and Threatening Communication (Scotland) Act 2012 has two sections, the first '*offensive behaviour at regulated football matches*' and the second, '*threatening behaviour*'. Following in the tradition of banning orders, searches, drink bans, passport controls and other targeted forms of regulation faced by football fans, the new law only applies to football supporters. As Tony Evans, the *Times* football editor, recently noted, 'People attending matches have to suffer assaults on their civil liberties on a weekly basis. In almost any other walk of life, these restrictions on individual freedom would cause a national uproar' (*Times* 19th March 2012). The Offensive Behaviour Act followed in this fine tradition.

In the rhetorical promotion of the act by SNP politicians, it was the nature of the behaviour, in particular its 'sectarian' nature, that was promoted as the problem. However, as a *law* defining a new *crime*, the act needed to specify what crime was being committed. When challenged about this, MSPs like Humza

Yousaf would reiterate that this was not a speech crime; it was only a crime if the words and actions of fans were likely to create a public order offence.

The act explains offensive behaviour as behaviour:
- likely (or would be likely) to incite public disorder.
- expressing hatred of people based on their:
    a] *Religious group,*
    b] *Social or cultural group,*
    c] *Or a group defined by colour, race, nationality, ethnicity, sexual orientation, transgender identity or disability.*
- that is threatening.
- that a reasonable person would be likely to consider offensive.

So it is not enough to simply sing a song and be arrested for it because this would not necessarily imply a situation likely to *incite public disorder*. Or does it? In section five of the first part of the bill, the point is made that public disorder may be likely if we take into account that there are 'measures in place to prevent it'. In other words, if the police were not at games, and other safety measures were not in place, would this offensive behaviour by fans lead to public disorder? First of all, this appears (as is the case with public order law in general) highly speculative. How do you know that public disorder would occur? As there are hardly any arrests at or after games, why should we assume that it would? And as many arrests are likely to take place days after the event – when no public order issue has occurred – will this not disprove the public order problem? I suspect it will not. Added to this, of course, is the reality that football fans may act in a particularly aggressive and offensive manner precisely *because* the police, security staff, cameras and partitions are there in the first place. They know that there can in fact be no public order problem. In other words, they have no intention of committing an act of physical violence themselves, and they know there is no chance that a bruising opposition supporter has any chance of getting at him or her for singing an offensive song. The presumed volatility of football supporters and the assumption that fans are potentially violent, especially the rowdies who sing and shout offensive songs in an aggressive manner, means that the public order or disorder issue becomes a given. Following the logic of this clause in the new act, the authorities could argue that the very presence of the police means there is already a public order problem. Consequently, any aggressive form of chanting and behaviour by fans can be interpreted as a criminal act if the officer present deems it to be so.

The 'likely to incite public disorder' clause also acts as a fig leaf which gives the act legal potential and credibility but which has little need for proof. As a colleague noted, it smacks of Kafka plus Minority Report, an unquestioned tautology enforced by the full power of the state and based around presumptions about what fans *may* do in the future – a future filled with images of violence and disorder in the minds of ministers and police chiefs.

In correspondence with a Glasgow-based lawyer who deals with many football related charges, I explained that MSPs like Humza Yousaf assured me that the law would only be used if a genuine public order issue was evident. 'Your assurance from the MSP', the lawyer explained, 'is, I am afraid, worthless'.

A prison sentence of up to five years can be given to anybody found guilty of this offence, but it must be football related and must be associated with a specific game, with you being at this game, going to it, or watching it on TV, for example, in a public place. The type of 'behaviour' they are talking about, in terms of what may cause this 'public disorder', is physical action but also *things said*. Coupled with the definition of offensiveness that includes, *other behaviour that a reasonable person would be likely to consider offensive*, we have the criminalisation of just about anything said at a football game. The impact of this law will, of course, entirely depend upon the levels of policing at games, the priority given to finding these 'offence criminals' and on the political pressure and climate that encourages the police to up their game at certain times and against certain sets of supporters.

The 'reasonable person' protection appears as little protection at all when it is the police who will have the discretion to arrest people and sheriffs who will decide what this 'reasonable person' is. At a time when the government has made it clear that no reasonable person sings 'sectarian' songs, the outcome of this act is to further reinforce an environment where incorrect speech associated with football is made criminal.

Those defending the act constantly fell back on the public disorder clause. There is no free speech issue, they argued, there must be potential public disorder as well. As we have seen this 'public disorder' defence is almost meaningless given the way in which football fans are perceived and treated and the way public disorder has become an imagined thing rather than something that actually happens or is likely to happen.

Concern was raised by civil libertarian voices within the parliamentary discussion about the potential threat to freedom of speech presented by the bill. The government had already specified that the new law would not affect poets, performers, comics and so on. Nevertheless, they were encouraged to amend the bill to allow for 'discussion or criticism', 'expressions of antipathy', 'proselytizing' and the 'urging of adherents of religions to cease practising their religions'. As long as sectarianism was carried out by 'civilised' people, like artists, or in a 'civilised' manner, by preachers and the like, it appeared to be fine. In this respect, the new law was not simply opposed to certain kinds of speech, it was opposed to certain kinds of speech carried out in a certain way, in a certain place, by certain types of people: rowdy working-class football fans. This was both a speech and a behaviour crime, specifically targeted at a particular group of people in society. The discriminatory nature of it is breathtaking.

Discussing the lawmakers' decisions to 'target Scottish football fans', Kevin McKenna argued that the act meant that 'Scotland's commitment to the human rights of its own citizens has now become a little tawdry and diminished' (*Observer* 18th December 2011). Similarly, Iain MacWhirter, outraged by the act, explained that:

> *Outlawing the singing of songs at football matches seemed such a ridiculous proposition that initially I thought the Scottish Government weren't serious. That Alex Salmond just wanted to 'send a message', and that the loopier parts of this unnecessary legislation would be dropped. And if not, MSPs would realise that such a law is as unworkable as it is objectionable. Surely, reason would prevail. It hasn't* (*Herald* 15th December 2011).

The second section on *threatening communication* targeted material which implies a threat, is likely to cause a reasonable person to suffer fear or alarm, and which purposefully intends to cause fear or does so through recklessness.

One of the better critics of the bill, MSP Patrick Harvie, in the stage three briefing discussion, observed that this measure for what was seen as threatening communication and consequently a criminal offence lacked rigour and was too open to interpretation. He explained that:

> *I can say* [that the test for criminality is not tough enough] *from experience of the one time that I was charged with breach of the peace following a demonstration at Faslane, when two burly police officers testified that they were caused great fear and alarm by the fact that I was sitting quietly in the road. 'Fear and alarm' is often used in a loose way and I am concerned that this will happen in relation to this offence.* [40]

Having already seen the eight months imprisonment received by Stephen Birrell for being offensive on the internet, a form of offensiveness that the Sheriff accepted was not 'threatening', it is unclear why this part of the act was needed. Nevertheless, Harvie's concern appears to be well founded, as should be our own concern that the test of 'reasonableness' and also of 'fear and alarm' are simply left to the police and criminal justice officials themselves to decide upon, and to use as the basis of prosecutions.

Discussing what should and should not be seen as offensive in this act, during the second stage discussion of it, Labour MSP Michael McMahon raised a concern about Rangers and Celtic fans celebrating their traditions in a way that some people may find offensive. What, he asked, would happen if people found offence with Scottish politicians celebrating their own bloody history, their battles and victories over the English, for example? Could this not be experienced and understood by somebody as something that was offensive, perhaps even threatening? Jeanette Findlay, chair of the Celtic Supporters Trust, has argued that chants about the IRA were 'songs from a war of independence going back over a hundred years' (*Daily Mail* 21st November 2007). No doubt Rangers fan groups could argue similarly about their own songs and chants. For the Scottish government however, some traditions, it seems, are more acceptable than others.

Conclusion

The question remains about why the Offensive Behaviour Act came into existence given all the laws that were already in place to punish football fans behaviour and words. One significant reason, which we will discuss later, is the importance of anti-sectarianism for the new Scottish elite. Like anti-racism in England, anti-sectarianism is a great issue to grandstand over, an unquestioned good which gives moral authority to whoever stands on the pulpit and shouts down the sectarian hordes.

The new law was also heavily supported by chief police officers who helped drive not only the legislation but the rhetoric about the sectarian and violent problems facing Scottish society. As we will go on to see, new criminal categories like 'Old Firm domestic violence' were constructed and promoted by the police. They also pushed for a zero tolerance approach and appeared keen to develop their new football policing unit and surveillance equipment. The levels of policing of fans in Scotland, especially Old Firm fans was already oppressive. With the prioritisation of the problem of offensive fans backed up by the new law, this is set to escalate to new heights, with the police acting as offence takers and seekers trawling the stands, the pubs and the internet to shamefully unearth 'Scotland's Shame'.

The new law evened things up regarding Old Firm 'sectarianism'. Before this act was passed Celtic fans could legally challenge the attempt to charge them with sectarian offences. Once passed, IRA and other politically 'sectarian' football songs could be targeted in the same way that racial or religiously aggravating songs could be. This criminalising of political songs and banners was rarely raised as an issue by the government, perhaps because of the clearly authoritarian and anti-democratic nature of this development.

The new law was in many respects, nothing new, but following in the trend to criminalise words. The difference was more in the open ended framing of 'offensiveness' – something which many liberal commentators found disturbing. Unfortunately, these same liberals had either ignored or supported the criminalisation of religious and racial words and backed the laws that laid the basis for the Offensive Behaviour Act. This is something that sociologist Carlton Brick warned may happen. Writing in 2000 he argued that, 'Once one class or area of speech is criminalised others are immediately brought within the boundaries of illegality, or become questionable'.[41] Brick noted that:

> While the criminalisation of other types of speech such as chants, songs and expressions of emotion associated with football may not be the intention of the advocated of the regulation of hate speech, it is without doubt a possible outcome.

And so it has turned out.

From a criminological perspective, a fascinating if depressing aspect of these new laws developed in Scotland is the extent to which previously radical political issues of the 1980s have mutated into matters of policing and regulation. Political and social issues of equality have been transformed into a more psychological discussion about 'hate'. Ironically, one of the outcomes of this development is that racism, and arguably sectarianism as well, loses, rather than gainS weight and significance as social and political problems, and simply become other forms of antisocial behaviour – of impoliteness. Brick notes this, arguing that, 'Through the construction of the notion of hate speech, the issue of racism has been recast as a problem of the way people speak and behave. In effect, racism has become de-politicised'.[42]

The public order aspect of the Offensive Behaviour Act is largely a legal fig leaf to cover up the reality that this new law represents a further extension of the policing of words and thoughts in Scotland. The prejudiced way in which football fans are treated and policed, coupled with a presumption of violence associated with offensive words sung by fans, means that supporters simply have no defence against the charge that their songs, chants and heckles are a public order issue. The outcome is likely to be that young working class men, like their counterparts in the United States, will increasingly be burdened with criminal records and extended prison sentences, some for simply shouting words that the authorities find offensive.

4

New Snobs v's White Trash

Certain types of people and forms of behaviour cannot be hated, but it is fine to hate other kinds of people and behaviour.

FRANK FUREDI, *ON TOLERANCE*

THE ISSUE OF OFFENCE, OFFENSIVENESS AND BEING OFFENDED HAS GROWN exponentially in recent years, shifting concerns and forms of regulation away from a collective public order issue or a race only related concern to incorporate ever more types of behaviour that are deemed to be unacceptable. In this context, not only football fans but football players as well have found themselves in all sorts of difficulties. Expressions of hate, or what are defined as expressions of hate, are no longer acceptable – unless of course that hatred is directed by the new elite towards the 'reactionary' white working class.

I'm offended

Despite the clear preoccupation with Scotland's sectarian 'shame' that led to the creation of the Offensive Behaviour Act, offensiveness in and of itself became the basis of the actual law. This is something which fits into a wider trend across the UK, both within football and in the wider world. At the same time as the Offensive Behaviour Act was being passed in Scotland and the police were already upping the surveillance of fans, in England a complaint was being made by the Football Supporters Federation and other human rights groups about Tottenham Hotspur football stewards using head-mounted cameras to monitor fans. In response to these complaints, a club statement was released explaining that the 'comfort and safety' of supporters was paramount and that fans should remember that 'foul, abusive, homophobic or racist language will not be tolerated at White Hart Lane' (*Telegraph* 21st December 2011). Here, the types of 'behaviour' that Tottenham Hotspur Football Club deem to be offensive extends beyond racist and even homophobic language to include 'foul and abusive' words. The importance of preventing this offensive behaviour necessitated the monitoring of fans with head-mounted cameras.

More generally, there has been much concern raised on radio chat shows and by sports columnists about the problem of offensiveness at games. Stan Collymore on *Talk Sport* is convinced that there is a growing problem of offensiveness amongst fans and has himself received racist remarks on Twitter that have been investigated by the police. In the North London derbies between Arsenal and Spurs, alternative forms of outrage have been shown by both sides. Harry Redknapp, for example, described a 'sick song' directed at Emmanuel Adebayor about a shooting in Angola as something only people who were not right mentally would sing, exclaiming, 'There were kids up there' (*Metro* 2nd October 2011). Matthew Syed, the ex-England table tennis international and *Times* journalist denounced the 'vile chants', that expose the 'hatred' at the 'heart of game'. In particular, Syed's concern was about the chant aimed at the Arsenal manager which goes, 'There's only one Arsène Wenger, One Arsène Wenger, with a packet of sweets and a cheeky smile, Wenger is a paedophile'. 'Shocked?' Syed asked his readers, 'Good' (*Times* 5th October 2011). For Syed, the singing of this song represented something of importance, something detestable; it represented hatred, not on the sidelines or amongst the few, but at the very heart of the game. Syed resisted calling for laws to stop this but felt that every other measure was needed to prevent this offensive behaviour.

Outside concerns about racism, concern about 'paedo' chants aimed at the Arsenal manager appear to top the list of outrage articles about football chants in England – perhaps because Arsenal are the team most courted by the 'Guardian-reading' football fan. Marina Hyde, writing in that same 'liberal' paper, explained with outrage that the chanting by 'knuckle-dragging cretins' who mock Arsene Wenger 'needs to be silenced' by the authorities (Guardian 3rd September 2009). Writing in the Daily Mirror, Oliver Holt has argued that a number of unacceptable fan chants about Munich, Hillsborough and paedophiles mean that the 'FA and police must come down hard on disgusting chants and abuse'. We may point the finger north of the border at Celtic and Rangers but England has its own problems, Holt argues. Arrest people for singing these songs, he demands. 'Things would change then, I promise you, and English football would be able to look itself in the mirror again instead of turning away in embarrassment' (Daily Mirror 26th April 2011). Football fans, it seems, are a constant source of 'embarrassment' to certain sections of society.

Even Sir Alex Ferguson has come out and asked his own fans to stop singing paedophile songs at Wenger. Concerned about Wenger's 'suffering', Ferguson argued that these chants go 'way beyond any legitimate form of terrace humour'. Thankfully, Sir Alex has not asked for the police to come and arrest his own fans for singing these offensive songs. Not yet anyway.

Listening to these comments you would think that football had suddenly become foul mouthed and offensive, that children at games are only now hearing unpleasant comments about opposing fans, or that sick chants about players and managers emerged only recently. Songs about the Munich air disaster are not new, nor is the tone of many of the chants which are purposefully insulting, cruel, infantile and depending on your sense of humour, funny. In 1978, after Rangers player Tommy McLean committed suicide, to the tune of 'Where's your Mama Gone?', Celtic fans (and others) would sing, 'Where's your Tommy gone – he's left his engine on'. In a similar vein, after Celtic's Johnny Doyle was electrocuted in his home in 1981, to the tune of 'It's my party and I'll cry if I want to', Rangers fans (and others) sang, 'It's my attic and I'll fry if I want to'. Some people may have found these songs offensive at the time, but there was little or no public outrage expressed about them nor attempts to get people arrested for singing them.

What appears to have changed is not the offensiveness of fans, but our expectations of what players and managers and even fans are expected to put up with or to be able to deal with at matches. With this has come a desire, even a campaign, to have offensiveness banned from games, regulated by stewards and even criminalised and acted upon by the criminal justice system. In the past you may have got some old worthies talking about 'public decency' and the 'national disgrace' of fan behaviour, but this was a minority conservative preoccupation. Today's 'outrage' is different in terms of the more widespread nature of it, but also in terms of the victim-centred anxiety about the harm being done by offensiveness. It is also far more inclined to result in calls for the police to deal with this 'problem'. Some complaints about blaspheming football fans may have been made by elite individuals at the start of the twentieth century, but today what it means to be a blasphemer is not related to God, or to the undermining of society's moral standards, but about saying hurtful things and causing alarm or offence.

One interesting aspect about so called offensive songs today is that they are actually far less overtly violent in content. Past songs were often directly about getting your 'fucking head kicked in', for example, and there were many similar songs that celebrated violence and directly challenged opposition fans to a fight. Today, the 'offensive' songs in question rarely imply any threat of violence and are often chirpy wee ditties rather than aggressive, finger pointing, two fingered screams at the opposing crowd. And yet, it is today that we are profoundly offended by these chants?

Old Firm offended
The concern, reporting of and expectation of action to stop offensive songs has grown in Scotland over the last decade. This has taken the apparently political form of targeting racism and sectarianism, but has emerged more significantly within the framework of 'offensiveness'. Note, for example, the way in which the discussion around the Offensive Behaviour Act was openly discussed as a law to tackle 'political sectarianism' by Chief Police officers but by few if any of the politicians proposing the law. Rhetorically, the new law was a political 'fight against bigotry and sectarianism', but in content and in law it was about offensiveness. In other words, it was less about challenging political or religious ideas than it was about controlling unpleasant words. Part of this process involved the growing engagement with 'offensiveness' by the authorities, but also a growing public form of complaint expressed in terms of, 'I'm offended'.

In 2008, for example, a Celtic fan wrote a letter of complaint to the Irish Embassy in London about the 'Famine Song'. This complaint was then passed to the Scottish government and Rangers Football Club produced a statement explaining that they were attempting to discourage their fans from singing the song and that they had discussed the matter with Strathclyde Police.[43] By September of that year, Celtic's chairman John Reid condemned the song as racist and in breach of race relations legislation. In November 2008, the first Rangers fan to be charged and found guilty of racially aggravated breach of the peace for singing this song occurred after a match against Kilmarnock. By 2009 it had been officially defined as racist by Lord Carloway.

In relation to the first case in November 2008, it was Rangers stewards who acted against twenty-year old William Walls. Nicola Tait, 24, said that one of her tasks as a steward was to monitor the Rangers support for sectarian behaviour, including the singing of the 'Famine Song'. Tait said that her instructions were to take the seat numbers of those guilty of sectarian behaviour and report them to Rangers for further action. Finding Walls guilty, Sheriff McDonald told him that 'given the whole context' his conduct was 'likely to be generally alarming and very disturbing to others' (*Daily Record* 26th November 2008). As it happens, looking at the report of Walls's behaviour, it could certainly be argued that he was being a bit of an idiot. But, then again, fan behaviour at games is rarely what one would describe as rational or polite. The focus in court, however, was less about the disorderly behaviour itself but the specifically-defined offensiveness and 'racist' nature of the song.

The case against Rangers songs being defined as racist and discriminatory was given a boost by UEFA in 2006 when they overturned their own decision and ruled that Rangers fans had sung discriminatory songs in their matches against Villarreal. Despite Rangers Football Club protesting that they were involved in initiatives to combat sectarianism and racism, this was not seen as good enough and a fine of £13,300 was placed on the club. Initially, UEFA had explained that this was an issue in Scotland and needed to be resolved within Scotland, despite article five of their disciplinary regulations stating that, 'racist, discriminatory, politically extremist or insulting' conduct will not be accepted. A spokesman for Scotland's leading anti-sectarianism organisation, *Nil By Mouth*, described the original UEFA decision as bizarre and outrageous, noting that, 'This is a shaming judgement for the whole of Scotland...the overwhelming majority of people in Scotland, including the chairman of Rangers, think it is completely unacceptable to sing songs about being "up to our knees in Fenian blood"'.[44]

The discussion about the 'shameful' Rangers fans that followed the initial UEFA judgement, coupled with the final decision to fine Rangers because of their fans 'Billy Boys' song, accelerated the move to discipline songs that were seen to be discriminatory and offensive. Today, Rangers make announcements before every game about fans desisting from singing sectarian and offensive songs and a number of these songs are no longer sung.

Part of the pressure to ban or regulate these songs came from Celtic Football Club. However, as we mentioned earlier, they too have come under scrutiny from UEFA for their own brand of 'offensive' songs. After their Europa League tie with Rennes, Celtic were reported for 'illicit' (whatever that means) chanting. They were subsequently fined £12,700. What was most interesting about this event was that it was a senior police officer, Eddie Smith, who had complained to UEFA about the songs being sung. Smith made a similar complaint to the Scottish Premier League and was also the main prosecution witness in a case against two Celtic supporters charged with sectarian breach of the peace for unfurling a banner with the word 'Huns' on it.

Again, it is clear that these songs sung by opposing Old Firm fans are not new. What is new is the desire and action being taken to regulate and criminalise songs that are defined as being particularly offensive, including, in the latter case of Celtic songs, those which include the term 'Hun' and others that include mention and support for the IRA. Like Rangers Football Club before them, Celtic F.C. denounced their own fans for singing these songs.

The meaning of offensiveness is expanding. Even in terms of what is defined as racist or sectarian, the number and type of songs being targeted by the football authorities and the police has grown in recent years. Terms that people may have frowned upon in the past have become relabelled as *offensive* – once given this high status the door is opened to further action by the authorities. The '*Famine Song*' is an example of the expanding use of the label 'racist', while terms like 'Fenian' have for some time been defined as sectarian and bigoted when used by Rangers fans. Historically, Celtic fans have argued that Rangers songs are sectarian (specifically anti-Catholic) whereas Celtic songs are political (for example, singing Irish Republican songs rather than shouting 'Fuck the Pope' as some Rangers fans do). Unfortunately, for Celtic fans, under the auspices of offensiveness, the political or religious nuances of chants have become irrelevant; all that matters is whether your song can be defined as offensive by the authorities.

The end result of all of this, and of the Offensive Behaviour Act, is that fans in Scotland can now be arrested and charged for singing any song that is deemed to be offensive by what the police and politicians define as a 'reasonable person'. Indeed, the act has a specific clause which specifies this very point. As we have seen, there is supposed to be a public order issue for arrests to take place. But as certain songs are defined as offensive – and as under the Public Order Act it is already seen as an offence to cause alarm, harassment or distress to an individual – then in essence you can be arrested for doing nothing other than singing offensive songs.

In a strange twist of fate with regard to the above discussion about 'shocking paedo chants', at the time of writing, one of the first people to be found guilty under the new act is a 25 year old Rangers fan, Lorne Macleod. His crime was to call Celtic fans 'paedophiles'. Perhaps a new category of 'sexual sectarianism' needs to be added to this expanding list of offensive terms?

From harm to offence
The extent to which words are being policed today and treated as criminal offences in and of themselves should not be underestimated. From John Terry to the Suarez-Evra affair and even the racist tweeting by the Swansea student who subsequently received eight weeks in jail for writing offensive comments about Fabrice Muamba, it has become an accepted norm within the realms of football to police, regulate and even imprison people for saying unpleasant things. In England this often takes the form of 'tackling racism'. In Scotland, this discussion often relates to the 'problem of sectarianism'. However, in both cases, the list of offences and offended keeps on growing.

This is not simply a football issue, and new laws in both England and
Scotland have developed to target 'hateful' words across society. In addition,
existing laws are being reinterpreted in order to police and criminalise an
increasing array of words and behaviours. Studying the *Criminalising of Free
Speech*, Alex Bailin observes that this trend can in fact be seen across Europe. In
contrast, free speech in the United States remains, to some extent, protected by
law. For example, a group in England who protested against returning British
soldiers and shouted comments like 'baby killers', were recently convicted
under the Public Order Act 1986. This was despite having followed police
instructions about their protest and despite the police having done nothing to
prevent the chanting. No public disorder occurred but the ruling noted that the
words used were 'potentially defamatory and undoubtedly inflammatory'. But,
Bailin asks in relation to the question of free speech, is it the role of the criminal
justice system to prevent this type of speech? As he notes, 'since protest by its
very nature is directed at an unsympathetic audience, it is very likely to inflame
and antagonise'.

Similarly, a British National Party member who displayed a poster in his
home window proclaiming, 'Islam out of Britain – Protect the British People',
was also found guilty of a public order offence. Rather than being overturned by
the European Court of Human Rights, the appeal was declared inadmissible on
the basis that it concerned an attack on a group based on their religion. Bailin
lists a number of other cases where charges have been made but eventually
dropped, for example the case of a teenager who was arrested for holding
a placard with the word 'cult' written on it while standing outside the Church
of Scientology.[45] Back in Scotland, we find that in Glasgow an American
Baptist evangelist, Shawn Holes, was fined £1,000 for telling shoppers in
Glasgow that homosexuals were bound for hell. The gay activist Peter Tatchell
called this an 'attack on free speech and a heavy-handed excessive response to
homophobia' (*Spectator* 30th March 2010). More generally, regarding religious
views being expressed in the UK, a recent report exploring this issue, *Clearing the
Ground*, argued that the rights of religious people to express themselves freely
had been disregarded in the name of laws that supposedly promote equality.

If the Public Order Act 1986 is being used more flexibly to criminalise a wider
set of words and behaviours, more recently the British government passed the
Racial and Religious Hatred Act 2006. This made it an offence to 'stir up racial
or religious hatred'. Here, the incredibly woolly term 'stir up' replaced the more
robust, previous category of incitement to violence, once again making many
more words and forms of behaviour criminal. Likewise, under the Terrorism
Act 2006, the connection between words and actual violence has been collapsed
further through discussion of 'indirect encouragement of terrorism' and the
new criminal offence of 'glorifying' terrorism. This latter act does not require
any proof of any danger of an actual terrorist act being, or in the process of
being, committed. Simply by 'glorifying' terrorism you can be imprisoned

– which raises further questions about possible charges that could be made against IRA or UVF chanting at games.

In contrast to all of this, American rulings in similar situations of offensive demonstrators have argued that, 'the irritating, the contentious, the heretical, the unwelcome and the provocative, provided it does not tend to provoke violence' should not be made illegal. Speech may be painful, as the American Supreme Court has noted, 'but we cannot react to that pain by punishing the speaker'. Furthermore it was noted that, 'freedom only to speak inoffensively is not worth having', and that the First Amendment of the American Constitution extends, 'to protect even hurtful speech on public issues to ensure that we do not stifle public debate'.[46]

For the Americans, the harm principle established by nineteenth-century liberal John Stuart Mill remains an important aspect of what it means to live in a free society. On the issue of judging the criminality of speech, there must be 'clear and present danger' created by the speaker – a situation where there is a direct connection between the words spoken, and the potential for physical *harm*. In Scotland, the UK and indeed across Europe, the link between words and potential actions has become so broad as to be almost meaningless. In many respects, what we see now with football fans is the straightforward policing of their offensive words. Today it seems that the 'correct' form of governing is one that attempts to protect people from emotional harm rather than simply physical harm, from words as well as deeds. As philosopher Joel Feinberg has noted:

'We have moved from the harm principle to the offence principle'.[47]

Class hatred

There has been a lot of discussion about hatred in Scotland in the last decade and perhaps especially in 2011 when the SNP government promoted the need for the Offensive Behaviour Bill. However, one aspect of hatred in society that is rarely if ever discussed is the hatred or at least the contempt that the political and cultural elites have for the working class, perhaps especially the white working class and specifically, white working class football fans. Past elites had an old-fashioned snobbery about football fans and an anxiety about the potentially violent mob who packed into stadiums every Saturday afternoon. The new elite on the other hand rarely express overt contempt for the 'lower orders' but nevertheless have maintained this old conservative anxiety and have added their own prejudices about the imagined underclass of sectarian, racist, sexist and homophobic football fans. In their imagination, the hordes of supporters are a pogrom waiting to happen.

This view of football fans is not isolated to Scotland. Indeed, following Alex Salmond's summit to 'fight sectarianism' in Scottish football, British Prime Minister David Cameron followed suit in 2012 and called his very own summit. This time it was to tackle 'racism and homophobia' in English football. Ironically, just as the Scottish summit had kicked off following trouble on

the pitch rather than in the stands, Cameron's reason for the race summit
came following the incidents between John Terry and Anton Ferdinand and
the handshake refusal between Luis Suarez and Patrice Evra. Despite this, the
outcome will be a further intensification of the regulation of the behaviour of
not only players, but more particularly the fans themselves.

Cameron's stated concern was that football should not get dragged back to
the 'bad old days' when racism was more widespread at grounds. Why name
calling by a couple of players should lead to such a statement and summit was
not explained. Neither was the fact that the summit mutated from its original
concern with racism to incorporate homophobia as an issue to be tackled in the
game. The presumption, of course, is that football fans have every prejudice
under the sun. So, if we're looking at racism, why not homophobia as well? As
with the issue of sectarianism in Scotland and racism in England, homophobia
was simply assumed to be a problem amongst players and the working-class
men who go to games. This assumption was not based on any serious evidence
about gay players suffering or about a rise in homophobic chants; it was
simply a given – an elitist expectation of what this class apart are like. This is
not to argue that there are no homophobic chants at football games, but the
sudden interest in this by Cameron and the English Football Association tells
us more about their prejudices than it does about the problem in the dressing
room or on the terraces. In fact, a Stonewall survey – 'Leagues Behind' – carried
out in 2009 found that two-thirds of fans, when asked, said they would be
comfortable with openly gay players playing for their team. More generally,
social attitude surveys suggest that homophobia is significantly less prominent
in society than it was a generation ago. Arguably, both racism and homophobia
have never been less of a problem in society, and yet the prime minister of
Britain feels the need to 'take a stand'.

This prejudice about football fans is illustrated very well by the politically
correct content of the Offensive Behaviour Act. Here, we have almost every
group in society that is seen to face discrimination included in the categories
of people to be specifically protected by the new act. Colour, race, nationality,
ethnicity, nationality, sexual orientation, transgender and disability were all
identified as needing special protection, something that was welcomed by the
Equalities and Human Rights Commission. Perhaps I haven't been to enough
football matches recently but I can't recall the infamous disabled or transgender
football chants! Of course, implicit within this section of the act is, again, the
presumption that football fans need special awareness training to overcome
their prejudices. This is the reason that politicians, the police and sheriffs keep
justifying their severe sentencing of fans with the note that, 'This will send out
the message that this type of behaviour is not acceptable in a modern Scotland'.
With each high profile trial ending with this statement, the enforcement
of law becomes as much about awareness raising, about correct forms of
behaviour, as it is about dealing with individual criminal acts.

In England, a profoundly contemptuous view of fans was illustrated during the discussion about the Tottenham and Bolton fans' reaction to Fabrice Muamba collapsing on the pitch. Rather than presuming fans would respond in a humane way to this tragedy, commentators more often than not expressed their surprise. Patrick Barclay in the London *Evening Standard* confessed to 'pleasant surprise at the alacrity with which fans of Bolton and Tottenham united in wishing or praying for Muamba's recovery' (*Evening Standard* 19th March 2012). Mick Dennis of the *Daily Express* similarly stated that, 'We were thankful that football supporters behaved properly for once because frequently some do not'. Dennis was expecting fans to 'chant something foul' as the medics came on to the pitch because fans, apparently, 'are getting courser' (*Daily Express* 20th March 2012). The inability of these commentators to realise that football fans would act in a decent way when a man was dying on the pitch in front of them tells us an awful lot about where the main problem of prejudice in football lies.

The social commentator Mick Hume rightly wondered:

Why, for example, did so many observers feel moved to congratulate the Bolton and especially Spurs supporters for their 'dignified' and 'civilised' response, after the crowd spontaneously came together to sing Muamba's name and then quietly left the stadium as the match was abandoned? Only because the authorities and much of the media now consider the mass of football fans to be such lowlife scum that they were shocked to discover the crowd showing such humanity.[48]

This case is redolent of how the police could only assume that the opposing Nottingham Forest fans who came onto the pitch to help the dying Liverpool fans during the Hillsborough disaster were about to cause a riot. These modern-day commentators are left dumb struck by the fact that when it really matters, football fans don't boo, jeer or throw bananas onto the pitch but applaud opponent players and fans and act in an entirely civilised way. The cages that used to surround pitches may have been pulled down but the loathing and contempt for working-class football supporters has not gone away. What has changed is the focus of policing. Today it is no longer our bodies and our actions that are controlled so much as our minds and our words.

White trash

It is no accident that the Offensive Behaviour Act is targeted at football fans and football fans alone. It is because football fans are predominantly working class. It is unimaginable that any other section of society could be targeted in such a way; again, this is not simply a football matter but reflects the wider prejudices of the political and cultural elites about 'white trash'.

In the 1970s and 80s, sections of the old elite hated and feared black working-class youth whom they saw as a criminal class of inner city muggers and illegal immigrants who were undermining our decent law-abiding British culture and way of life. Key sections of today's cosmopolitan elite have flip-flopped and their class prejudices are now reserved for the white working class who they see as undermining our multicultural Britain. Overt elitism is less acceptable today and up-front contempt for 'scum people' or the 'lower orders' is often veiled behind talk of 'white van man' or 'Sun readers'. Talk about 'football fans' in certain circles has itself become a euphemism for white trash, and indeed when those in authority and in the media discuss the problem of racists, homophobes and those who carry out acts of 'domestic violence', we all know who they are talking about.

Contemporary comedians avoid like the plague any jokes that could be seen as racist. Almost all right-thinking comedians avoid discriminatory jokes of any kind; of any kind, that is, except those about Neds, Chavs, shell suits and so on. Go to the Edinburgh Fringe Festival and listen to the up and coming comics trying their hand and you'll soon find the reliable old joke about the pregnant teenage chip eating Chav. 'Am I bovered', asks Catherine Tate's Lauren Cooper? 'Yes but no but' replies Matt Lucas's Vicky Pollard. Comedians should, naturally, be able to crack jokes at anyone's expense. But just as the club comedians' racist jokes told us something about society thirty years ago, today's unashamed mockery of 'white trash' tells us something about today's prevailing prejudices.

It was noticeable that during the 2011 riots in England, the reaction to Asian men organising themselves against the rioters was relatively calm, even supportive. This contrasted to the panic and contempt expressed towards the white working class men in Essex who did the same thing. One left-wing newspaper talked with outrage about the 'mob of white men swarmed through the streets chanting "England"' (*Morning Star* 10th August 2011). The Metropolitan Police spokesperson called them 'vigilantes' who 'appeared to have been drinking too much'. Others talked of a 'white mob' and of a 'race war', of 'race hate' and 'fascists patrolling the streets'.[49] Consequently, a multi-ethnic riot had by the end of the week become a problem of the white working class who dared to organise themselves against the rioters. Responding to reports that the English Defence League had helped to organise against the riots, David Cameron having witnessed towns and cities being trashed and burned by rioters remarked that, in 'sick' Britain there is no group 'sicker than the EDL'.[50] As Brendan O'Neill pointed out: 'Note to the cultural elite: Just because someone is white and possibly a labourer and not currently glued to the American remake of *The Killing*, that doesn't mean he is a fascist'.[51]

The outrage and hysteria expressed across the press and by politicians towards one hundred or so men walking along streets in Essex singing England songs is illustrative of the fear and loathing that exists today amongst 'right-thinking' elite sections of society. Considering that there are hundreds of thousands of such people going to watch football matches every week, it is perhaps no surprise that the beautiful game is being swamped by ever more laws and initiatives to control their behaviour. In this context, the concern about 'offensive behaviour' becomes something very different from the civilising mission it is portrayed to be by those in authority. This explains, in part, why there is such an over-the-top reaction in society to petty displays of offensive behaviour, especially when it is carried out by this 'class' of people.

This is not simply a football thing. A regular feature of discussions about popular culture is a thinly veiled contempt for the working class, their crude materialistic tastes and their incorrect attitudes.[52] This was illustrated most clearly in the 'race case' involving caricatured Essex Girl Jade Goody in 2007. Here, the *Big Brother* contender found out to her cost the extent to which people being 'offended' could become a national and even international issue. After her childish name calling of 'Shilpa Poppadom', thousands of complaints flooded in to Channel 4 from the public, a denunciation was issued by the then Chancellor Gordon Brown and even the Indian Minister for External Affairs condemned Goody's behaviour. It seemed that almost everybody wanted to get in on this incredibly unimportant story to explain that they too found this behaviour offensive and unacceptable. The *Sun's* comments about Jade Goody: 'She has left the house with her true personality laid bare – a vile, pig-ignorant, racist bully consumed by envy of a woman of superior intelligence, beauty and class' just about summed up the vitriolic levels that this offence incident reached. It resulted in Goody going into hiding, receiving 24 hour police protection and even contemplating suicide (*Sun* 24th July 2007). This witch-hunt involved not only 'liberal' and tabloid commentators alike but race quangos and politicians. One spiteful columnist described Goody as one of the 'beastly slags' of the 'British underclass', and part of 'ugly thick white Britain'. The *Guardian* explained that her outburst reflected 'the stupid hatred of these white women for a brown one', something that revealed what happens in 'pubs and clubs most nights' (*Guardian* 19th January 2007). Jade Goody was described as an 'escapee from the underclass', that section of Britain that is 'shallow, stupid, ignorant and inherently racist'.[53]

Racist and sexist
A good example of the new reactionary form that elitism takes towards football fans, not just in the UK but across Europe, is the case of the panic surrounding the trafficking of prostitutes for the 2006 World Cup in Germany.

Before the German World Cup kicked off, the international feminist organisation Coalition Against Trafficking in Women, launched a 'worldwide campaign' about the abuse of prostitutes, noting in particular their concern that, '40,000 women will be imported into Germany from Africa, Asia and central and eastern Europe' for the competition (*Guardian* 30 May 2006). The charity division of the television music company MTV subsequently launched a global advertising campaign to highlight the issue of trafficking of women and girls for forced prostitution. The advert read, 'Still cheering? Thousands

of women and girls will be trafficked into Germany during the World Cup
and forced into prostitution. End exploitation and trafficking' (*Guardian* 9
June 2006). The unquestioned image of bigoted sexist football fans created an
international story based on the assumption that these drunken and abusive
men would soon be exploiting trafficked women on a mass scale.

This story was promoted by German Green MEP, Hiltrud Breyer, and by her
Austrian socialist colleague Christa Prets and the question of trafficking came
to dominate International Women's Day in Brussels. Some old conservatives
also got involved in the issue, with Anna Záborská, a right-wing Slovakian
Christian Democrat, challenging FIFA head Sepp Blatter to condemn
trafficking, noting that, 'After all, isn't it true that in the masculine world
football and sex go hand in hand?'. Germany was condemned in international
circles as the world's pimp, and Juliette Engel, director of the MiraMed
Institute in Moscow, argued that this was a case of 'the exploitation of
women's bodies and souls by tens of thousands of male football fans notorious
for their drunkenness and violence'. Even American Republican New Jersey
Congressman Christopher H. Smith got involved and explained that President
George W. Bush would be having a word with the German chancellor, as he had
'very strong views on this issue'.[54]

The problem of trafficking during the Germany World Cup was reported
as a matter of fact in the UK but the reality of the 'trafficking' situation was
very different to the presented problem. As Samuel Loewenberg reported
in an article in the *Lancet* entitled 'Fears of World Cup sex trafficking boom
unfounded', in July 2006, 'Although there are scattered reports of an increase
in prostitutes, it is nowhere near the 40,000 predicted by the newspapers,
and there is as yet no evidence of an upsurge in forced prostitution'. For
him, the trafficking panic and representation of a bonanza of sexual slavery
'seems to have been hysterical media hype'.[55] European correspondent, and
one of the few critical British commentators on this issue, Bruno Waterfield,
similarly noted, that despite the extra border policing, huge awareness raising
campaigns, and the setting up of a telephone hotline by NGOS, the prostitution
scare story 'turned out to be pure fiction'. With reference to a European Union
report on the subject, he explained that, 'the German police uncovered just five
cases of 'human trafficking' for the purposes of sexual exploitation related to
the football tournament'. There were also no cases of alleged forced prostitution
linked to the World Cup reported to the government funded helplines. Even
the expectation of increased customers for prostitutes appear to have been
exaggerated, with one newspaper noting that, 'the increase in the numbers of
punters which was forecast by some did not materialise and that was the reason
why some prostitutes left before the 2006 World Cup was over'.[56]

This trafficking example is illustrative of the problem we face in football if
we are to have a balanced understanding of what problems do and do not exist.
Unfortunately, as the twenty first century progressed, many 'radical' and

'tolerant' individuals rather than challenging old elitist panics about working class football fans were more likely to be at the forefront of those condemning these fans and demanding more policing and regulation of their drunken, violent and bigoted behaviour.

Wife-beating bigots!

The trend amongst the new elite to presume that working class football fans are bigots, and to automatically link this with a wider problem with abuse and violence in society is perhaps best expressed through the strange case of domestic violence. Like racism and homophobia – automatically associated with football fans in the heads of the authorities – the last decade has seen a concerted effort by the police in Scotland to make a direct link between wife-beating and Old Firm fans.

During the promotional stage of the Offensive Behaviour Bill, domestic violence was held up, with all the other issues, as a serious problem whenever the Old Firm played their games. When the *Joint Statement on Scottish Football* was initially launched by Alex Salmond in March 2011, domestic violence had already joined the roll call of problems associated with football fans alongside alcohol misuse, sectarianism and racism. Indeed, domestic violence received priority treatment within this statement – it called for the greater use of Football Banning Orders and the use of the clubs own codes of conduct to tackle the 'criminal behaviour of fans away from the grounds specifically domestic abuse'.[57]

In September 2011, the Glasgow *Herald* proclaimed a 'Warning over huge rise in Old Firm domestic abuse'. Figures 'unveiled' by the police showed domestic violence 'soared' (or 'rocketed' depending on which paper you read) following this particular Old Firm clash, with a 'hike of more than double the level on an average Sunday', the numbers of reports increasing from 67 to 142. In fact, this was an unusually high figure as the average increased figure after Old Firm games is around 107 and, arguably, as Scottish Women's Aid noted, this higher than usual increase may have been due to the high-level publicity given to the campaign. Tackling Old Firm domestic abuse, the police explained, was one of the key reasons they had pushed for the football summit in the first place and was why they and the Procurator Fiscal were taking a proactive approach to the issue. Before the game, there had been a promotional campaign about this issue and the police had also taken the unprecedented step of 'knocking on the doors of some 400 known perpetrators of domestic abuse over the weekend to warn them against violence and pursue outstanding warrants for minor offences'. Pictures of these police activities were shown on BBC TV news in Scotland. As a police spokesperson said: 'This is not just a set of statistics about crime in the west of Scotland on an Old Firm weekend. Behind every one of the numbers is a victim, a family and a community blighted by the violence that, sadly, is still attaching itself to this fixture' (*Herald* 20th September 2011).

A feature article written in the same edition of the *Herald* noted that this Old Firm game had been a good one in many respects as only a small minority of fans caused disruption and there was no repeat of the 'ugly' scenes between the managers of Rangers and Celtic like there had been previously. But this wasn't good enough for this commentator because, 'In one significant respect... last weekend was yet another dark one for football and its continuing struggle to free itself of its problems with violence, alcohol and religious hatred'. The problem was one of domestic violence: 'In other words, we may have taken a small step forward on violence in the stadium on Sunday, but the troubling link between the stadium and the home, where men turn their frustration at the scoreline into violence against their wives and partners, is as bad as it ever was'.

Christine Grahame, the convenor of Holyrood's Justice Committee, which was scrutinising the new 'sectarianism legislation', said that the focus should now be on 'what happens when the fans leave the stadium and go elsewhere and that is surely right even if it takes us all the way into the fans' homes...Now there has to be the same vigilance on the domestic as well as the sporting front if this poisonous problem of domestic abuse is to be tackled too'.

Here we had a fascinating situation where the reality of hardly any violence at Old Firm games was skated over and the focus now became the home of people who were having a domestic dispute. There appeared to be some connection with a Celtic v Rangers tie being played and an increase in complaints to the police. However, we do not know if the men involved in these cases were actual supporters of either Celtic or Rangers. Even if we assume this is the case, the figure for the worst increase is 75 reported cases, the usual increase being about 40. Again these figures have to be seen in the context of press, police and political interest as well as the additional resources thrown at the problem. It should also be seen in the context of the 2.5 million people living in Strathclyde and the potentially hundreds of thousands of people drinking, celebrating and commiserating after the game. These figures, it is worth reiterating, are reported cases, many of which will not relate to domestic 'violence' as such and most of which will not lead to arrests.[58]

More generally it is the case that there is a rise in domestic incidents reported to the police at other times when large numbers of people go out drinking and celebrating. Both Christmas and New Year see an increase of this kind, suggesting that it is more of a situation that arises from drinking and partying in general rather than anything specific to Old Firm fans. Even if we take the above figures as proof that it is an Old Firm fan involved in every incident, this is still a tiny minority of these hundreds of thousands of fans. Yet the labelling of the problem, the discussion about the 'soaring' levels of abuse and the warnings by the police to all Old Firm fans leaves no doubt that this is a general problem with these football fans.

It is worth emphasising the entirely constructed nature of the 'Old Firm Domestic Abuse' issue. For example, 1996 is the first year that the two terms

'Old Firm' and 'domestic violence' appear alongside one another in any newspaper. However, these articles were about Paul Gascoigne. It was in 1998 that the first substantive article using both terms appeared. Before this time, there was no direct connection made between the Old Firm and domestic violence. From then until the late 2000s, there was an average of five articles a year in all newspapers in the UK using these two terms. The issue of 'domestic violence' appeared rarely and, when it did, it was simply as one of a list of violence-related problems in Scotland. On the 31st March 2005, the first article of its type that directly connected the Old Firm with a specific statistical increase in domestic violence appeared in the *Sun*. Reported by Superintendant Harry Watters, it was claimed that domestic violence can almost double on Old Firm days. Possibly because domestic violence was an issue that the police were prioritising (in part to improve their image) and also reflecting the developing concerns of the new elite, it began to take a higher priority in the press and even at football games. In 2007, for example, the Old Firm began to show adverts about domestic violence at half time. In 2008, special police patrols were launched in Glasgow to crack down on domestic violence. A zero-tolerance approach to the issue has meant that, like race-related incidents, all domestic incidents must be logged by the police regardless of the evidence. In 2010, major police action, press releases about the issue, and new statistics 'proving' the link to the Old Firm led to 31 articles about this issue. In 2011, this had leapt to 325.

From a zero-tolerance perspective, 'one incident of domestic violence is one too many'. This sounds entirely reasonable. That there is an increase in offences after Old Firm games similarly creates a situation where campaigning about this problem makes sense. However, similar attention could be paid to rugby internationals, political events or even policeman's balls – anywhere where large numbers of people get drunk – and discover a jump in domestic incidents. But such attention is never shown.

By my calculation there were six Old Firm games in 2011. If we estimate that there was an increase of 50 reported domestic incidents for each game (which is actually far more than there were) then we find approximately 300 incidents of this kind in the whole year. Looking then at the 325 newspaper articles discussing the Old Firm and domestic violence in 2011, we find that there was more than one article for every single incident. In other words, there has been more than one article for every person who has been involved in any sort of reported domestic incident that might be connected to the Old Firm. If we assume that there are 100,000 regular Old Firm fans who go to watch the games at Celtic Park and Ibrox on a regular basis, and if we assume they are directly involved in these 50 domestic incidents reported after any given game, then we find 0.05 percent of match going fans involved in this problem. If we assume that there are around ten times this number of people who watch or take an interest in the Old Firm matches in Strathclyde, this figure becomes 0.005 percent.

On top of this, if we look at arrest statistics rather than reported incidents, then for figures provided by Strathclyde police regarding a midweek Old Firm fixture on 2nd March 2011, we find that the increase in domestic abuse-related arrests was three. So, for this week, the soaring problem of Old Firm domestic violence that led to arrests and necessitates half-time announcements at games, ministerial pronouncements, police initiatives and a mass of press articles, was 0.0003 percent of fans.[59] If a similar figure of offending and a similar level of press outrage, police activity and political rhetoric was geared towards a similar scale of problem over something like 'black mugging' it would be called an authoritarian moral panic. In 'modern tolerant Scotland' it miraculously becomes a cause for celebration, leading to ever more campaigns and policing of the bigoted white trash that Old Firm football fans are assumed to be.

It is true that there is an increase in people arrested on domestic abuse charges on Old Firm nights. It is also true that 99.9997 percent of Old Firm fans across the whole of Strathclyde do not go home after the match and beat their wives (or husbands, for that matter). That the new category of Old Firm domestic abuse has been constructed and now uncritically accepted as an established social problem in Scotland once again tells us very little about the prejudices of the knuckle dragging 'scum people', and an awful lot more about the reactionary prejudices of the new elite.

Conclusion

The Offensive Behaviour Act replicated many existing laws but broadened the discussion to focus on issues of hate and offensiveness. But, as we have seen, the question of hate needs to be turned on its head as the most powerful prejudices are actually contained within the elites themselves. This helps to explain why the language used in the debate about sectarianism often borders on hysteria and hyperbole.

The elevation of the incorrect use of language, as a political and sometimes criminal issue, automatically puts sections of the working class at a disadvantage, especially young men who are more often crude and rude than their middle class contemporaries. The use of this 'incorrect' language also leaves people open to the accusation of intolerance – a secular sin that connects them to all manner of wrong doing from racism to homophobia – and in Scotland, to sectarianism, to violence, and in the perfect storm – leads us to the inevitable construction of the bigoted wife beating Old Firm fan.

The policing levels at football in both Scotland and England are exceptional and fans have to 'suffer assaults on their civil liberties on a weekly basis' (*Times* 19th March 2012). However, the assault on freedom of speech should be seen as a more general trend that stretches across society, both in the creation of new laws and the increasingly flexible definition of public order offences which result in an ever-growing number of words and actions being criminalised. One especially worrying consequence of this is that the freedom to demonstrate, or even to prosthelytize, is being undermined by the actions of the state to protect people from offence.

Iain MacWhirter, writing in the Glasgow *Herald*, noted at the time that the Offensive Behaviour Bill takes the law into the subjective realms of hate crime. It will criminalise thoughts and behaviour that other groups find offensive. He went on to argue: 'Well someone should tell the First Minister and his MSP clones that the right to offend people is the most basic right in any democracy' (*Herald* 15th December 2011). He's right. Unfortunately, today the newly constructed 'right' not to be offended increasingly trumps all other freedoms.

One of the most ridiculous things about criminalising the offensiveness of football fans is that being offensive is part and parcel of supporters' behaviour at games. There can be few other areas of life where chanting, shouting, swearing, and singing highly offensive songs are part and parcel of the culture of that activity. At football matches grown men can often be seen acting in a profoundly aggressive, confrontational and tribal manner. In many respects, what is being attacked, vilified and even outlawed by today's elites is simply football culture itself. Today's fragile, rather nervous elites cannot see past their prejudices about the white working class to be able to see the pantomime that is taking place at games. Outrage can take the form of a demand to stop bigotry. But it can equally be expressed in shocked terms regarding paedophile chants or even the bad language of fans. This helps to explain how, bizarrely, one of the first uses of the Offensive Behaviour Act was to charge Rangers fan Lorne Macleod because he was calling Celtic fans paedophiles. Some offences are more easily criminalised than others, but the expansion of outrage and regulation is unremitting.

The great liberal philosopher John Stuart Mill, when explaining the true meaning of freedom of speech argued that, 'there ought to exist the fullest liberty of professing and discussing as a matter of ethical conviction, any doctrine, however immoral it may be considered'.[60] Football fans aren't really discussing a matter of ethical conviction or even attempting to have a discussion. But the principle should be the same. Unfortunately, the *offence principle* is fast becoming the one that dictates the way society is governed.

5

The 'Myth' of Sectarianism

We can never be sure that the opinion we are
endeavouring to stifle is a false opinion; and if we
were sure, stifling it would be an evil still.
JOHN STUART MILL, ON LIBERTY

IN SCOTLAND THE DEVELOPMENT OF LAWS TARGETING OFFENSIVE WORDS HAVE been developed most specifically in relation to the perceived problem of sectarianism. It is this idea of sectarianism more than anything else that has intensified in the last decade and led to an array of new laws and forms of policing targeted at football supporters. Unlike racism in England however, which is generally accepted to have been a problem in the past, there are questions about what this thing sectarianism in Scotland actually is and whether or not it even exists. Here we examine the question of sectarianism itself, not least of all to help illustrate once again the prejudicial way in which the discussion about offensive football fans has developed.

The sectarian problem

The problem of sectarianism is often exaggerated. The inflammatory type of language used in discussions about this issue suggests the problem is being inflated by some sections of society. At times, it is seen as an issue in Glasgow and the West of Scotland alone. At other times, it is marked as a wider Scottish problem. It can be represented as an issue that needs to be nipped in the bud before it spreads; at other times as something that is deeply ingrained in Scottish culture. It is also a problem that has become heavily associated with violence. Medical metaphors are rife, pointing to a 'virulent disease' that is 'infecting Scotland'. Emphasising (and exaggerating) the importance of sectarianism, David O'Connor, the president of the Association of Scottish Police Superintendants explained that the police should take a tough approach because 'sectarian behaviour strikes at the very heart of our social fabric in Scotland' (*Scotsman* 23rd November 2012). The late Catholic QC Paul McBride even argued that Scottish independence could have 'very serious consequences' for Catholics in Scotland as sectarianism could 'blossom' if Scotland were released from the influence of England (*Scotsman* 31st August 2011).

This idea that sectarianism 'strikes at the heart' or that it is 'at the heart' or 'at the centre' of Scottish culture, fabric or society is a deeply curious one. Problems that are central to society rarely need to be discussed in this way. For example, we don't need to use bombastic language to convince people that the current economic crisis 'strikes at the heart' of society, because it is obvious that this is the case. The clear need of the authorities to explain time and time again that sectarianism is hugely important suggests the opposite. Equally, and perhaps more importantly, one gets the feeling that each time a politician or police officer stands up and makes a statement about how important sectarianism is, what they are really saying is, 'I'm really important'. As we will discuss in the next chapter, there is a rather unpleasant narcissistic quality to anti-sectarianism, something that makes the discussion less about the issue itself and more about the person speaking about it. 'Look at me! I'm fighting against sectarianism.'

It is often unclear what is being discussed when concerns about sectarianism are raised. Historically, it is understood as a religious problem; but there are the additional, and arguably more important, political elements associated with Irish Republicanism and British Unionism. More often than not, the discussion ends up focusing on two things: football and violence. Indeed, the term 'sectarian' has become almost synonymous with the Old Firm and with drunken violent young men. The emphasis on the Old Firm can lead to complaints about Celtic and Rangers or the Scottish Football Association not doing enough to 'tackle sectarianism'. However, the centrality of football to the question of sectarianism should raise some doubts about this apparent social problem. What is it that is actually being discussed? Why, if sectarianism strikes at the very heart of Scotland's social fabric do we rarely, if ever, hear about this problem outside of the context of Rangers and Celtic football clubs? What type of 'serious' social problem only manifests itself when a football game is being played?

Despite the rhetoric about the cultural depths and significance of sectarianism, the fight against it is often represented as a police matter. For something that is understood to be a historic issue connected to belief systems and opposing ideas, churches, religions, wars and different countries, this legalistic and even technocratic way it is engaged with is strange. Roseanna Cunningham, discussing the problem as she saw it, noted that, 'We must deal with sectarianism in the same way as with racism, and drink-driving'.[61] The connection to racism suggests a political dimension to sectarianism; but drink-driving? There is a moral dimension to the drink-driving issue – it is wrong, bad, selfish, careless and thoughtless. But can sectarianism or 'religious hate', as they like to call it, be reduced to mere thoughtlessness? Cunningham no doubt means sectarianism, like drink-driving, should become unacceptable and be seen as morally wrong. But if sectarianism has any real substance or depth to it, surely it cannot be treated as simply another form of antisocial behaviour. It is hard to imagine, for example, that people fighting against communism or fascism in the past, or against Catholicism or Protestantism, would have used the 'fight against drink-driving' as their model. Ironically, this technocratic and depoliticised way of addressing sectarianism tells us a lot about the empty nature of the political elite. It also tells us a lot about the lack of political or even religious weight within Scottish sectarianism itself.

The myth of sectarianism

Steve Bruce and his colleagues have done Scotland a great service by writing *Sectarianism in Scotland*, in which they question the myth of sectarianism. Their evidence that Catholics in Scotland are not, and generally speaking have not, been discriminated against has faced little serious challenge from academics studying this subject.

Sectarianism in Scotland was written in part to look into the claims of individuals like composer James MacMillan who in 1999 argued that Catholics in Scotland were still seriously discriminated against. As we have already seen, the idea that sectarianism is rife in Scotland is rhetorically presented as a fact of life. But what is the evidence for this claim? What Bruce and his co-authors do is examine the issue of oppression and discrimination. Are Catholics discriminated against in the workplace, in politics and in unions? Are Catholics and Protestant living separate lives? Is religion an important feature of people's lives in Scotland? Are Catholics discriminated against in education and housing or cut off from mainstream Scottish society? Are Scottish institutions biased against Catholics? The answer they give to each of these questions is a resounding no.

Despite James MacMillan arguing that anti-Catholicism is 'as endemic as it is second nature', Bruce attempts to get some facts about this question rather than relying on what they see as a lazy connection made time and again between drunken football violence and the belief that this somehow represents a problem with Scotland in general. Exploring this issue historically, they argue that Scotland's past is more like that of the United States than Northern Ireland, where there has been significant institutional discrimination against the Catholic population.

Irish Catholic immigration into Scotland in the nineteenth century replicated what happened in America, and a Catholic community, often of poor working-class immigrants, emerged. With this wave of immigration, particular institutions and organisations, including Celtic Football Club, were formed. Despite these separate organisations and the existence of a Catholic 'community', through the twentieth century Catholics became integrated into the mainstream of Scottish society. Pockets of extreme anti-Catholicism did exist in the 1930s but political attempts to promote militant Protestantism failed. By this point in time, immigration had declined significantly and Catholics in Scotland were now native to the country.

In the 1920s, with the rise of the Labour Party, 21 percent of Labour councillors were Catholics – a figure proportionate to the number of Catholics in Scotland. Within the Labour Party and the labour movement more generally, there is little evidence that Catholics were underrepresented throughout the twentieth century – again something that cannot be said for Northern Ireland where discrimination against Catholics in the labour market was assisted by unions that privileged Protestants. This appears to be of significance given the importance of politics, political organisations and union power for systematic discrimination to occur.

Catholics were in worse-paid jobs in the early post-war period, possibly because of prevailing inequality and the fact that they tended to be from low-skill immigrant families. Over time, however, this disadvantage declined and for those who entered the labour market in 1980, there is no evidence for Catholic marginalisation. Nor is there evidence of discrimination by institutions like the police or criminal justice system. In all surveys on the question, there is a very small percentage of people who oppose inter-marriage between Catholics and Protestants – most of those who oppose it being elderly. Half of Catholics under the age of 35 marry a non-Catholic. Indeed, religion has been eroded considerably as a force in Scottish society and is less significant than it ever has been.

By 2002, 36 percent of Scots surveyed said they were 'Church of Scotland', 14 percent (and 24 percent in Glasgow) identified themselves as Catholic, and the largest number of people – 37 percent – had no religion. About half of those who identify their religion as Church of Scotland go to church less than once a year, while the same is true for 30 percent of Catholics. Young people under the age of 25 are far less likely to go to church than those over 55 years of age and, as Bruce and his co-authors note, young Scots simply do not regard religion as important. In terms of morality, the issue of sex before marriage is not a Catholic-Protestant question but a generational one. The Catholic Church may oppose things like abortion and contraception but Catholics – especially younger Catholics – do not. The Orange Order exists but is dwindling, despite an increase in membership during the Irish troubles. It is seen as religiously intolerant by the mainstream churches and has little by way of political support. In 1985, despite the conflict in the north of Ireland, the Scottish Unionist Party, who campaigned against the British government's agreements in Ulster, received only one percent of the votes in the three places it stood candidates for election. Anti-Catholicism, as Bruce and his colleagues note, is weak and extremely marginal in Scotland.[62]

This reality of the declining importance of religion, especially for young adults, appears to be most significant when considering that the vast majority of arrests, fines and imprisonment of people for religiously aggravated or sectarian offences will be from this age group. They may be labelled 'sectarian' by the press, police and politicians, but in a religious sense this label would appear to have no real meaning.

Three quarters of Celtic fans are 'Catholic' but this doesn't mean they are religious. Being Catholic is arguably more culturally significant than it is religious, part of this being an association with Ireland; however, only eight percent of Catholics in Scotland identify themselves as Irish, even when given the opportunity to choose from a number of identities. This is a smaller number than the actual number of Irish people who have moved to and live in Scotland.

Finally, when looking at the limited significance of 'sectarianism' in Scotland, in a Glasgow City Council survey of over 1,000 people, it was found that religion played virtually no part in terms of who respondents would prefer to have as a neighbour. Between one and two percent of people said the religion of their neighbour would be of relevance; most of those who said that it mattered were elderly. It is worth bearing in mind that this was a survey of Glaswegians, the place you would expect sectarianism to be more significant than anywhere else in Scotland. Yet hardly anyone cared about the religion of their neighbour.[63]

Is it really a myth?
According to James MacMillan, 'The West of Scotland is still basically a carbon copy of the north of Ireland, without the bombs'.[64] This is quite simply not true. That doesn't mean there are no prejudices in Scotland. Nor does it mean that individuals, and perhaps sections of the elites, historically held prejudices against Catholics. What it does mean is that in the twentieth century the Scottish state, and society as a whole, has not and does not systematically discriminate against Catholics. Certain private sector employers in banking and law, for example, are associated with the Masons and with anti-Catholic discrimination, but today there is little or no statistical evidence to show that this results in discrimination.

If there was systematic discrimination against Catholics in Scotland, one would have expected a reaction to it by Catholics themselves; it is unlikely that you would need academics to prove that it existed. You would expect to see a reaction as you did in Northern Ireland, but there has been no such reaction: There are and have not been any bombing campaigns in Scotland. If Scotland was a carbon copy of Ireland, where are the civil rights marches, the Catholic based political movements or even an armed struggle? And to mention it again, if sectarianism is a significant force in Scottish society, in housing provision, discrimination at work and so on, why on earth is there a preoccupation with sectarianism as a problem in football?

One reason that the Old Firm rivalry is focused upon is that the institution most recently associated with discriminating against Catholics is Rangers Football Club, who, for much of the twentieth century, would not play a Catholic in their team. This certainly reflected and upheld a Protestant ethos and the football club was arguably the most significant sectarian institution in Scotland. However, precisely because Rangers stand out like a sore thumb over their historical refusal to play Catholics in their team; this was an oddity rather than part and parcel of Scottish society. Criticisms of Rangers' sectarian policy mounted in the 1970s, in part reflecting the changing, 'liberating', times regarding morality, religion and indeed politics generated in the 1960s. By 1989, the policy was changed and Catholic player Mo Johnston signed for Rangers. The religion of players has been of no significance since then, suggesting perhaps that the weight of religious sectarianism surrounding Rangers, and certainly amongst the fans, was less significant than some people perceived it to be.

However, this is to dismiss the 'sectarian' issue of the 1970s and 80s too easily, without considering what the ACPOS Justice Committee submission called 'political sectarianism'. Bruce's argument about a lack of discrimination against Catholics is important. However, in terms of understanding the potential tensions and divisions in Scottish society, and the potential divisions embodied within the Old Firm, the limited time devoted to examining the significance of the Irish 'troubles' is puzzling. Looking at other writing on the subject of the Old Firm and sectarianism, this omission reoccurs. For example, in Bill Murray's *Old Firm*, the seventy pages looking at the 1970s and 80s give only a fleeting mention of the 'troubles'. This includes two pictures of a Loyalist leaflet handed out at Ibrox, promoting a protest, and a front cover of *Ireland's War*, the magazine of the Glasgow Irish Freedom Action Committee, promoting an Irish Freedom demonstration with the image of a masked armed man and the headline, '14 years of Irish resistance'.

Steve Bruce has rightly pointed out to me that in his study of Loyalists in Scotland there were only a few thousand people who could be seen as having an 'extremist' view on the issue of Northern Ireland. Indeed, as he notes, despite the political loyalties and even hatred that existed amongst a small minority of Scots at this time, not only were there no bombing campaigns, there were no killings carried out in the name of the 'troubles' from either side.

However, this would still appear to underestimate the importance of an issue that is seen by some as representing a virtual civil war within the borders of the UK. It, again, seems odd that in these books, almost no mention is made of the events at the time and the importance of them, not only for people in Northern Ireland, but for the UK population as a whole. Bobby Sands starving himself to death in a fight to re-establish the status of political prisoner, the bombing of the Conservative Party conference in Brighton, the wrongful imprisonment of the Birmingham Six and the Guildford Four, the killing – some believe, assassination – of three IRA members by the SAS in Gibraltar, the killing of Lord Mountbatten and so on.

It would be hard to overestimate the significance of the 'troubles' for the British government and British state in the conflict with Irish republicanism. For all the major political parties in the UK, there was a unanimous and unflinching determination to fight and win this battle. It was arguably the most important and explosive political issue of the time, one which animated the animosity between Glasgow's two biggest football clubs. It was within this charged context that Celtic flew an Irish tricolour above its ground while some of their fans sang IRA songs at games and bought copies of magazines sold outside the ground with pictures of paramilitaries on the front cover. Meanwhile, these fans faced 'Loyalist' opponents allied to Rangers singing the British national anthem and 'No Surrender to the IRA. We might see then that the issue of 'sectarianism' was anything but a myth; there may not have been a war in Scotland, but there will have been a distinct animosity amongst at least certain sections of both Celtic and Rangers fans. Added to this is the fact that thousands of Rangers and Celtic season ticket holders are from parts of the north and south of Ireland and many will have had strong opinions and allegiances regarding the conflict in the North.

Some academic and political discussions about the Old Firm attempt to find weight and meaning in 'religious sectarianism', locating the origins of contemporary rivalry by looking back to centuries of religious tension between

Catholics and Protestants. However, this surely overlooks the political conflict over Northern Ireland that gave some dynamism and substance to tensions and divisions within football and in parts of wider Scottish society. Indeed, this attempt to find an explanation for recent tensions as far back as the seventeenth century reflects a profoundly conservative approach to history and people. It sees identity emerging out of the soil of history or from 'stories passed down through the generations', rather than in the far more real economic, social and political tensions of the day. For example, without conflict in Ireland, it is unlikely that Rangers would have held onto their backward 'no Catholic players' policy for so long.

Despite the occasional opprobrium and distain expressed towards Rangers regarding this no Catholics policy, while British troops were 'at war' with the IRA, the tendency was for the conservative elites to turn a blind eye. Not only that, but when Rangers faced Celtic on the pitch, the British establishment would know very clearly which side they were supporting: It wasn't Celtic. As long as the conflict remained, fervent loyalty to the Union was a positive thing for the political elite and Rangers would have been the establishment's team of choice. Whether or not this effected the way the different sets of football fans were policed is open to debate. It is also possible that the political tension at the time would generate some anti-Catholic violence.

For most people in Scotland, even in Glasgow, it is unlikely that this issue led directly to violence, it was nevertheless an extremely important political and military conflict within the context of recent British history. It is worth emphasising that this conflict over the Union and over Irish independence was a *political* conflict that involved the British state; it was not an issue of 'sectarianism' driven by religion, bigotry or the uneducated stupidity of the working class, as is so often the assumption about 'sectarianism' today.

Given this, it is difficult to get a grip on the importance of 'sectarianism' in the 1970s and 1980s, or what should perhaps more usefully be called political tension and rivalry. Whatever the reality, Bruce is right to note that this is not and never was like Northern Ireland, especially in terms of violence, or in terms of people's ultimate political loyalties being formed around the Irish question. Also, the Labour Party and the labour movement in Britain and Scotland, both Catholics and Protestants alike, were in the main pro-British, or at least anti-IRA, when it came to the issue of Irish independence. Consequently, there was no significant divide in Scottish society, as there was in Northern Ireland, which needed to be controlled by the authorities. Even in terms of the republicanism expressed at Celtic games, this remained a minority interest; for the majority it was largely a ninety-minute football affair, rather than something which determined fans' wider social, public and political life.

The most important point to note for this book is that whatever the tensions in the past, today, the war is over. There are no 'troubles' as such and there is no Irish republican movement. Consequently, what was by far the most important issue for encouraging rivalry and tension between different sections of Scottish society, and even within football, is of no significance except as a historical legacy. It is something that may be remembered in songs but not something that can mobilise hearts or minds, of even a minority of Rangers or Celtic fans, to do anything other than support their football team.

Not only is Irish republicanism no longer a movement and the conflict something that those under the age of thirty are unlikely to remember, but British 'loyalism' is itself not what it was. The unity of the British state is itself peacefully up for discussion in terms of Scottish independence. Traditional symbols of Britishness like the Royal Family are as often mocked today as they are celebrated, and overt signs of Britishness are often treated as a problem by the British state itself. This is the main reason that Rangers fans find themselves in the strange position of having gone from being the establishment's team to finding themselves pariahs to the new cosmopolitan elites.[65]

The confused notion of sectarianism

Sectarianism is part of the furniture of Scotland, an ever present reality of life. Or so it is assumed to be. When discussing the issue, politicians or academics are rarely required to define exactly what this thing sectarianism actually is. In law there is no set definition of this problem. In terms of the word itself, sectarian simply refers to sect-like behaviour, defending or supporting your narrow group or outlook against those of other people. Being sectarian, in many respects, is the opposite of being cosmopolitan or multicultural; it takes little interest in the 'other' or turns its back rather than embracing it. Sectarianism could be challenged as being narrow minded or exclusive; it could also be defended as an outlook or set of beliefs that should be free to exist in what is, after all, meant to be a multicultural society. You surely cannot have a multicultural society without different cultures.

However, sectarianism is rarely challenged at the level of ideas. It is often portrayed as an issue to do with religion and bigotry, but this is not part of a discussion about the nature of religion. When sectarianism is discussed as a religious issue it is simply to label it as a form of bigotry and/or violence that can be dismissed and condemned – never discussed. Despite the attempt to deal with sectarianism at this level (for example, the introduction of section 74 of the Criminal Justice (Scotland) Act 2003 which created the aggravated offence motivated by 'religious prejudice') academics generally recognise that 'sectarianism' is not largely driven by religion. For young people in particular, religion has little or no relevance or significance for their lives. As we have seen in the Glasgow City Council survey, for most adults, religion is irrelevant when deciding where to live, and all social attitudes surveys indicate that there is no sectarian divide when it comes to the issue of marriage. Even when we look at the high profile 'sectarian' cases, where we might imagine some fanatical sect-like family creating fervent bigots, we often find that the person deemed to be acting in a sectarian manner has relatives from across the 'great divide'. The Facebook offender Stephen Birrell has a Catholic mother, for example. Could religion be a serious driving force for this thing 'sectarianism' in the twenty-first century? Are the few Rangers and Celtic fans who fight each other upset about one another's scripture? Clearly not.

The issue of Catholic schools has not been addressed here and, as the most important religiously-based set of institutions, it deserves a mention. From this author's perspective, schools should be free of religion, but that doesn't mean that Catholic schools necessarily create a sectarian Scotland. As we have seen, all the indications are that Scotland is not a religiously-divided nation, and it is becoming more secular all the time. Catholic schools increasingly appear to be places people want their kids to go, not because they are Catholic, but because they often have a better reputation as good schools. Nevertheless, it is interesting that despite all the talk about sectarianism, the Scottish government seems to tiptoe around the issue of Catholic schools or ignore it completely. The rather feeble attempt to 'bring kids together' has been tried, with shared campuses and playgrounds, but no government has seriously addressed the issue of Catholic schools. If, as the political elite seem to believe, sectarianism is a genuine problem in Scotland, surely this would be one of the first issues on the agenda. Yet it is not.

Politics would appear to be a better place to start when looking for 'sectarianism'. The conflict in Northern Ireland was arguably the most important issue the British government and state had to face in the late post-war period. This conflict potentially breathed new life into old 'divisions' amongst sections of Scottish society. Even out-with the 'extremists' of both Loyalist and Republican camps, there was a potential tension based on sympathy or antipathy towards Ireland as a nation and towards the Catholic community in the north of Ireland in particular. The tension over Ireland has historical roots, but the conflict in the 1970s and 1980s could have given fresh impetus to this tension and did become the backdrop for many of the songs, chants and symbols used at Old Firm games to show your support for your team and hatred of your 'enemy'.

The ACPOS Justice Committee submission raised the issue of 'political sectarianism', something they clearly saw as key to the rivalry and ill feeling at games. But the point about this political tension is that it too is of little or no relevance today. The conflict in Ireland is no longer the tense battleground it was, either politically or militarily. There is no longer war in Ireland. In this respect, there is no political basis for sectarianism; no living breathing everyday experience or issue driving a potential divide. Some people may hold onto their beliefs from the past, some may even use the Old Firm games as a way to relive their past passions or anger. But even for these supporters, the songs and symbols represent a ghost from the past, rather than a live political problem in the present.

The myth of sectarian violence

Sectarianism in Scotland is often associated with the problem of violence, so it is worth looking at this question first of all. As we saw in a previous chapter, the murder of Mark Scott was important for those promoting the need to up the fight against sectarianism and it became part and parcel of the way that sectarianism became synonymous with serious acts of violence. Promoting the need for new laws to fight sectarianism back in 2002, and helping to form the way sectarianism would be discussed in the future, Liberal Democrat MP Donald Gorrie explained that sectarian violence was a 'cancer' that needed to be purged. As if providing a template for future rhetoric, Gorrie argued that sectarianism was a problem that was 'at the heart of Scotland', it was a disease, and as with diseases, and especially cancer, it could spread with devastating consequences for the entire body. Indeed, without serious forms of treatment, it is likely that it would get worse. But was sectarian violence a serious problem that justified the level of political and media attention it received at this time and which led to a new law being passed in the Scottish Parliament?

It is interesting that Mark Scott, who was killed in 1995, became an emblematic figure in the fight against sectarian violence in the first two decades of the following century. After all, if serious sectarian violence and murders were a significant or growing problem that needed a new law to stop them in Scotland, one would have assumed that by the time the 2003 law was introduced his name would simply be one of many that would trip off the tongue when discussing this problem. Yet his name stands out because it was untypical, extreme and rare rather than because it reflected a typical example of life in 'sectarian Scotland'.

The book *Sectarianism in Scotland* is especially useful when attempting to examine the real nature and extent of sectarian violence at this point in time. The authors, Steve Bruce, Tony Glendinning, Iain Paterson and Michael Rosie are again worth a mention because of their incisive attempt to go beyond the often hysterical reaction and rhetoric around this issue. For example, when addressing the extent to which Scotland can be seen as a mini Ulster, in terms of the armed violence that existed in Northern Ireland in the 1970s and 80s, they note only one known occasion when a large consignment of arms was shipped from these shores to Ireland. In the end, this 'inept' attempt was stopped by the police. Active, paramilitary activity in Scotland, even at the height of the troubles, appears to have been minimal, and families like the Campbells, and individuals like Jason Campbell who killed Mark Scott, are far from typical.

More importantly, *Sectarianism in Scotland* examines the issue of sectarian murders in depth and discovers a constant misrepresentation and exaggeration of this problem. Noting *Scotland on Sunday*'s 'screaming' headline in 2001, 'Stop Glasgow's Killing Fields', Bruce describes the issue of sectarian murders as a 'moral panic'.[66] In this newspaper article, *Nil by Mouth* founder Cara Henderson described her first Old Firm game, noting that, 'nobody was murdered within hours of the final whistle, a state of affairs provoking surprise among the Glasgow constabulary, which has grown wearily accustomed to weeding out killers from both communities – but especially the Protestant sector'. As Bruce noted, 'this was an interesting display of the ability to sustain a preconception in the face of refuting evidence'. It is also perhaps a useful reminder of the dangers of relying on the prejudices of the police to inform one's own practices, and also a warning about the potentially prejudicial opinions of 'victims of crime' who end up being given an influential position by government and the state in resolving these 'problems'.

However, there have been sectarian murders in Scotland. Examining these murders in an academic journal, James Conroy identified 11 between 1995 and 2002, more than one a year. This figure Bruce observed became, according to *Nil by Mouth*, 'Eight murders with a sectarian element in the last few years...an issue that shouldn't be minimised'. This figure was reported in the *Daily Record*, the *Herald* and was presented to a Justice Committee at the Scottish Parliament.

The original source for this statistic came from a report written by Elinor Kelly and Gregory Graham which identified 11 'Old Firm' related murders between 1984 and 2001 (rather than 1995 – 2003). In this same time period, there were 2,099 homicides in Scotland. Therefore, according to this report, sectarian murders made up 0.5% of the total. A Church of Scotland report looking at this issue had also mistakenly reduced the length of time to seven years, and then *Nil by Mouth* reduced it further still to just two years. Bruce and his co-authors look further still at these confused figures and assess the validity of even Kelly and Graham's figure of 11 murders in 18 years to find that only six can be labelled as sectarian (even here some of those amongst the six could be said to be definitely Old Firm related and only possibly sectarian, in my opinion). Using the figure of six murders in 18 years, this reduces the sectarian murder rate, as a percentage of homicides in Scotland, down to 0.3 percent.

Looking at homicides in Scotland as a whole, Bruce suggests it would be more helpful to understand the problem as one that is related to aggressive young men under the influence of drink or drugs rather than attempting to see these deaths through the prism of sectarianism. In this respect, and with reference to the six potential sectarian killings, they conclude that these murders are more a reflection of these wider social problems, including the carrying of knives, than some kind of endemic sectarianism.

Getting onto an important aspect of the confusion about 'sectarian violence', Bruce raises the issue that what we may be witnessing when we see this violence is not sectarianism at all, but football-related antagonism. Put simply:

> Imagine that the Old Firm vanished (as did all memory of them) and their places were taken by two teams – Glasgow East and Glasgow South – that had no ethnic or religious ties but that were extremely popular and regularly competing for the same prizes. Do we think that the level of violence would be markedly lower? [67]

One reason Bruce and his co-authors believe the violence would not be very different is that, 'Old Firm games are not unusual among local derby matches in generating violence'. They cite cases such a Manchester derby where large groups of City fans, some carrying smoke bombs, attacked United fans. Or another case where hundreds of rival Sheffield fans clashed, resulting in police use of CS gas and batons to restore order. When we get the arrest data for Old Firm games between August 2000 and December 2002, there was an average of just 12.3 arrests per game.

The exaggerated discussion about sectarian violence which mushroomed at the start of the century set a template for how this issue would be discussed from then on and has subsequently been used to justify a variety of police initiatives and increased police numbers and activities. Discussing violence in society or on estates can grab the attention, but not in the way that talk of 'sectarian violence' can.

Looking at a typical set of annual statistics examining the problem of 'sectarian violence', as it is defined, across the whole of Scotland, Steve Bruce noted in the *Scottish Catholic Observer* that:

The vast majority of offences are for relatively minor incidents – 92 percent being for breach of the peace, the aggravation in these cases being largely verbal. Half of those arrested were drunk and a third of those 'abused' were the police. Fourteen percent of the offences were associated with football games and 15 percent were on Orange marches.

Consequently, the 'reality of Scotland's sectarianism becomes clear'. As Bruce argues, 'The typical case is not a bigot searching for members of the public to assault: it is a drunk shouting at the police and others trying to discipline his uncivil behaviour'.

In terms of urban disorder more generally, Glasgow has for many years had a reputation for street gangs. Generally made up of school-aged children, these teenage 'gangs' are not grounded on religious allegiance or even on football loyalty; they are almost always territorial. In my previous life as a youth worker, this was exactly how things played out in Coatbridge, with Celtic and Rangers kids from different areas standing shoulder to shoulder in what was generally a mock battle with the other 'side'. Sectarianism, in whatever form or which ever way you want to define it, didn't even define the fighting habits of these kids or their basic loyalties as they grew up.

An alternative perspective on the Rangers and Celtic games and the rivalry between the two clubs might be one that dismisses the shock and horror and recognises that, as with football across the UK and indeed across much of Europe, you get some men who drink, get drunk and act like idiots. This is not new, but nor is it some monstrous problem – a plague ravaging Scottish football or society. Indeed, a more balanced representation of Rangers and Celtic would recognise and celebrate the passion, excitement, colour and life which these great teams bring to Glasgow and indeed to Scottish sporting life and culture as a whole.

Conclusion

If sectarianism is a myth, why is it still a recognised issue in Scotland? In the Glasgow City Council survey, a majority said that they thought sectarianism was a current and prevalent problem. Similarly, during the promotion of the Offensive Behaviour Act, the SNP kept citing their own research which indicated that the vast majority of people saw sectarianism as a problem and believed that something needed to be done about it.

Why does the belief in this problem persist? At one level, the issue is real. There are different religions in Scotland, there are Orange Lodges and marches; there are Catholic schools; there are terms like Hun and Fenian used by people, often, although not always, as a form of insult. But is this enough to make sectarianism a recognised social problem? Bruce and his co-authors again note that, despite only one percent of people in a Glasgow survey having experienced sectarian violence over a five-year period, two thirds thought it was a problem of some significance in general. Perhaps, they suggest, the myth of sectarianism and sectarian violence is maintained by newspaper headlines about 'Celtic fan stabbed', 'attack after Old Firm game' which imply a sectarian motive in acts of violence that have nothing to do with sectarianism. Anti-sectarian groups have an interest in exaggerating the problems and so do politicians. Even the Protestant Kirk, they note, repeats incorrect sectarian 'facts' to absolve itself of past wrong doing. More generally, as we will discuss below, anti-sectarianism, like anti-racism, has become a new moral prerogative. To deny the problem is to be a blasphemer, while to stand up against it is to be a 'right-thinking person'. Consequently, if you oppose the myth of sectarianism you run the risk of stepping outside of the 'correct' camp and of being labelled a bigot. The political focus on sectarianism undoubtedly raises its profile as an issue; coupled with this, the apparently bigoted, aggressive and macho rivalry of the Old Firm goes against accepted social norms today. Additionally, at a time when few powerful forms of identity remain in society, the passionate flag-waving fans of Celtic and Rangers appear increasingly alien to Scottish, middle-class sensibilities. Whatever the explanation, there is no doubt at all that the problem is exaggerated today through tawdry headlines about 'killing fields' that equate sectarian murders in Scotland to the millions killed in Cambodia which is not only ridiculous but also inexcusable.

The story of sectarianism fits many of the prejudices of the elites and middle classes today, prejudices about the nature of the white working classes in particular whose behaviour is out of control. As such, it is almost always associated with violence, and increasingly with other 'incorrect' forms of aggression, like domestic violence. And of course, in terms of West End dinner party etiquette, Old Firm football fan behaviour is 'out of control' – it is loud, crude, and rude and can be extremely offensive.

Time and again the discussion about sectarianism is focused on football fans, with their chants and songs used as evidence of the problem of bigotry in Scotland. However, this is to confuse a game with the real world; to misinterpret the pantomime of football with the problems of society. This is a mistake. To take fans at their word is silly. To assume that IRA or Fenian blood songs genuinely mean these fans want to kill one another is no more or less true than it is for any other group of fans across the UK. You may get some passionate Loyalists in the crowd, or some ardent old Republicans, but these will be a small minority, and simply because they have strong beliefs does not make them necessarily prone to violence. For the rest of the 50,000 football fans, the duration of their 'sectarianism' is a mere 90 minutes before they troop off home to their Catholic wives, Protestant work mates and non-denominational drinking buddies. You may get a few 'nutters' or some kids who want a fight, but this is not driven by the spectre of sectarianism, except perhaps for the 'sectarianism' of football fandom. In this respect, all football fans are guilty as charged. To be a football fan is to be sectarian.

I have suggested that in the 1970s and 80s there may have been an increased tension between Celtic and Rangers fans because of the Irish issue. It is also possible that the authorities treated Celtic fans, or the Republican element of them, with more opprobrium at this time. However, it is also noticeable that the songs fans sang were not an issue at this time – even though the IRA were bombing the mainland. In fact, in discussions with fans who went to games at this time, it appears that there was less rather than more policing of games. Police reports in 1976, for example, rather than suggesting an anxiety by the police regarding Old Firm matches, are far more measured and even relaxed about the fixtures, and the level of violence at games is compared 'favourably' with other groups of people who go out on mass and enjoy themselves on a Saturday night.[68] In contrast with today, there was arguably a maturity about the authorities then, who recognised that this was just a game, and that these chants and songs meant little or nothing in the real world – at least not in Scotland. Perhaps the elite of old were simply more worldly and able to recognise that the sectarianism shown at Rangers and Celtic matches was nothing more than football sectarianism.

The troubles in Ireland were unquestionably important for the British establishment. However, the potential tension this could have created at a political level remained just that – potential. Support for Irish republicanism, especially for the armed struggle, remained marginal even amongst the Celtic-supporting Catholic community in Glasgow. In this respect, the lack of importance given to this conflict by writers like Bill Murray is understandable and the core tension between Rangers and Celtic arguably remained just that, a football tension.

Writing in 1994, the year the IRA called a ceasefire and ultimately declared an end to the conflict over the question of sovereignty in Ireland, Simon Kuper published *Football Against the Enemy*, a book celebrating the great rivalries in world football. Here Kuper sees the battle between Celtic and Rangers as in essence

a football thing – a rivalry that excited and attracted fans from around the
world. Observing what he saw as a largely symbolic sectarian front presented
by the rival fans, he argued that, 'They are not about to give up their ancient
traditions just because they no longer believe in God'. For Kuper, the rivalry
between Rangers and Celtic was not unusual; theirs was not a peculiar religious
or politically-driven hatred. In general, observing the nature of fandom across
the UK, rather than simply in Glasgow, he notes that, 'British fans enjoy fan
culture, and most of all they enjoy hating their rivals'.[69]

In 1999 the academic Bert Moorhouse commented on the myth of
sectarianism. These songs they sing are part of the history of the clubs, he
observed, adding:

> They don't, however, reflect the reality of living in Scotland where society is not divided on
> religious grounds. Catholics and Protestants work together, live together, are even married to
> one another without it being an issue. These are the same people who sing these terrace songs...
> There is a kind of imagined adversity because sectarianism in life has decreased to a huge extent.[70]

Of course, football fans love the rivalry; they play up to it, mouth off about it,
make up new songs and wave their scarves to wind up their opponents. Hating
your local rivals is one of the joys of football. To take this rivalry, this 'hatred', at
face value is infantile.

Looking at the issue of current day *sectarianism in Scotland*, Steve Bruce sums it
up nicely:

> Most Scots are not football fans; most fans do not support Rangers or Celtic most Rangers
> and Celtic fans are not religious bigots. That some Rangers and Celtic fans wind each other up
> by falsely claiming to have strong religio-ethnic identities which are offended by the equally
> false religio-ethnic identities of the other side is not reason for the rest of us to take such ritual
> posturing as the basis for judging the polity, society and culture of an entire country (Observer
> 24th April 2011).

One of the most interesting things about the question of *sectarianism in Scotland*
is that it has become more of a political issue at precisely the time when
it means less and less in society, at both a religious and political level. The
evidence for sectarianism provided to us by the politicians and by anti-sectarian
campaigners does not relate to discrimination in the workplace or oppression
by institutions; nor does it relate to the strength of religious beliefs or teaching;
nor to political ideologies and organisations. It relates to abusive comments
shouted at games, terms exchanged with someone you are having an argument
with, threats typed online or something shouted during a drunken fight. *Today
sectarianism is largely a problem of name calling*. There is no social, economic, religious
or political depth or dynamic to it. Unfortunately, for both Rangers and Celtic
fans, name calling, or what has become known as 'being offensive', has become
the new original sin.

6

The Anti-Sectarian Industry: Intolerant 'Tolerance'

My duty to be tolerant towards the 'other'
effectively means that I should not get too close to
him, intrude on his space. In other words, I should
respect his intolerance of my over-proximity.
What increasingly emerges as the central human
right of late-capitalist society is the right not to
be harassed, which is a right to be kept at a safe
distance from others.
SLAVOJ ŽIŽEK, VIOLENCE

IN 2005, THE ACADEMIC TOM DEVINE QUESTIONED STEVE BRUCE'S ATTEMPT TO challenge the idea that sectarianism was a serious problem in Scotland. He argued:

Bruce reminds me of a scholarly Canute, standing firm and resolute as the waves of contrary opinion gather around him. Those who believe sectarianism is a continuing problem in parts of the country not only include the Scottish Executive, the First Minister and all the churches, but organisations as varied as the Association of Chief Police Officers, the Commission for Racial Equality, the Scottish Council for Voluntary Organisations, all political parties and all TV, radio and print media – and this is by no means an exhaustive list (Scotsman 16th February 2005).

But the fact that increasingly in the twenty first century Scottish institutions organised themselves around the problem of sectarianism does not prove that sectarianism is the problem it is represented as. If what the authorities believed was always understood to be simply the truth we would still believe in witches, or believe that black people are genetically inferior, or that women are simply different and the home was the place for them to be. Elite prejudices take different forms at different times, but in each time period their outlook is often the outlook of society itself. To list elite institutions and their views as proof that these views are correct is about as uncritical an approach to a subject as one can imagine.

This chapter looks at the growing obsession with anti-sectarianism at a time when 'sectarianism' at either a religious or political level is at its lowest ebb for generations. Religion is of little significance to people's daily lives in Scotland, and the political tensions that existed around the conflict in Ireland are of little if any relevance today. Consequently, the important thing to explore when looking at the political storm around sectarianism is not the sectarianism of punters on the terraces but the anti-sectarianism of the elites.

The question of tolerance is an important one in helping us to understand the ways that anti-sectarianism has grown and grown in the last decade. As the sociologist Frank Furedi has pointed out, the meaning of tolerance has been transformed. Having previously been the bedrock of the defence of free speech and the need to 'tolerate different beliefs and opinions', it has now come to mean the very opposite of this. Consequently, free speech has become regulated and criminalised as part of a process of enforcing 'tolerance of others'. Rather than respecting people's freedom to speak their mind, we are encouraged to respect people's differences and not upset them by saying 'offensive' things. This new right *not* to be harassed, even verbally, becomes the basis of new laws; at the same time, there is a vast expansion in the policing of language, thoughts and behaviour that were previously seen as of no significance or something that grown adults were expected to be able to deal with. As the public comes to be seen as vulnerable and in need of protection from offensiveness, 'intolerant tolerance' comes to the fore.

In the same way that racism has become an issue campaigned around and promoted throughout football at precisely the time when racism itself had already declined within society, in Scotland the 'fight against sectarianism' did not grow legs at a time when religion and religious conflict was suddenly flourishing amongst a new generation of adults. On the contrary, it occurred precisely at a time when religious dogma has never meant so little to young adults. Likewise, anti-sectarianism did not become a campaigned-about concern in Scotland while the war in Ireland raged, while bombs were being planted, while Loyalist paramilitary forces grew in the six counties or when members of the British government and the royal family were being killed by the IRA. It happened at the very time that this political and military conflict evaporated. In other words, at the time that chants of IRA have no meaning in the real world, and when songs about Fenian blood have no religious depth or significance, the Scottish elite bravely went on the offensive against 'Scotland's Shame'.

The strange rise of anti-sectarianism

To many ordinary football fans in Scotland, especially but not exclusively the Old Firm fans, the 'war' against sectarianism in football seems utterly bizarre. For these fans, especially the older fans, five years in prison for singing a song is unfathomable. More than this, the very fact that a song at a football match can lead to your arrest is treated with complete incomprehension. Nevertheless, this is the state of play today. In Scotland at least, much of the criminalisation of football fans has come in the guise of the fight against sectarianism.

Anti-sectarianism has become part of the fabric of life in Scotland, not just in politics, law, and football, but also in education. In schools, anti-sectarianism is now described as something that is at the heart of the new Curriculum for Excellence. 'Education,' the Scottish government notes, 'can play a pivotal role in challenging sectarian attitudes and religious intolerance'.[71] As such, anti-sectarian initiatives are crucial for developing 'informed responsible citizens'.

It is not only children who need awareness training about sectarianism. In prisons this attempt to develop 'positive attitudes' was given a boost in 2011 when the funding for anti-sectarian training of prisoners was doubled. The success of this re-education process would be judged by illustrating the changed behaviour of those receiving the training. For example, prisoners would be encouraged to understand that cracking sectarian jokes was harmful, something that it was claimed had been successful in 50 percent of cases so far (*Scotland on Sunday* 25th September 2011). By November of 2011 it was announced that anti-sectarian training would also be available for the staff of the Scottish Parliament (*Herald on Sunday* 20th November 2011).

To be against sectarianism is a new norm in Scottish society, an unquestioned good, something that can unproblematically become part of school curriculums and the training of prisoners, even parliamentary staff.

Sectarianism is also something that all politicians in parliament oppose and indeed something that has come to be vocally denounced by Scottish governments for the last decade. As Ruth Davidson, the Scottish Conservative leader explained at a debate in parliament, every single one of her MSPS is opposed to sectarianism.

At one level, opposition to sectarianism can be seen as a good thing. But to understand what is going on, we have to ask why now? Why and how has being against sectarianism become the new moral absolute, the new good, and something that the authorities feel needs to become part and parcel of all of our education?

Looking back at press coverage about sectarianism and the Old Firm from the early 1990s, what is fascinating is that the problem of Old Firm sectarianism was barely mentioned until 1997.[72] Sectarianism at Old Firm games was simply not a political or significant pubic debating point mentioned in the Scottish broadsheets before this time. From only two articles on the subject in 1992 and 1993, in the latter part of the 1990s there were around 40 articles each year on the Old Firm and sectarianism. There was then a doubling of the number of articles in 2001 and a peak of interest in 2002 with 117 articles on the subject. Old Firm sectarianism remained of some significance until 2006 and then declined. In 2011 following the SNP's campaign a new high of almost 200 articles were written about this 'problem' – one hundred times more articles than had been written in 1992.

What is most interesting about the rise and fall of interest in this issue was that it was not any rise in sectarianism that created it, but rather it was the rise in anti-sectarianism as a political, public and campaigning issue that generated the interest in sectarianism and the Old Firm. One way to describe this could be to say that the behaviour of fans did not change, what changed was the behaviour of the political elite. In essence, the Scottish authorities became less tolerant of Old Firm fans' behaviour. From an issue that attracted little or no political interest, it became one of the most campaigned around issues in Scotland.

Aspects of this change can be witnessed by studying the changing attitudes of individuals. One example of this change can be seen in the approach taken to Old Firm sectarianism by the celebrated Scottish sports writer, Graham Spiers. Writing in the *Scotland on Sunday* back in 1996, Spiers challenged the exaggerated idea of bigoted football fans in an article entitled, 'Glasgow's sectarian image doesn't bear close scrutiny' (*Scotland on Sunday* 14th January 1996). Insightfully observing the middle class preoccupation to go on and on about sectarianism, Spiers notes that:

> In Glasgow, in the pubs and wine bars and especially around the hearths of the chattering classes, you wonder if we can't let go of the tough subject-matter of bigotry. You wonder if some of us would feel stripped naked if we couldn't continually hark on about this "hate-filled" city of ours. For a community that has made great strides in softening the divide, too many of us crave the expression of a bygone era.

His own colleagues in the press were his next target of attack as he explained how, 'We lay thick the heaving vocabulary of hate and venom and rancour, and before you know it word is back on the streets of the further disfigurement of society wherever Rangers and Celtic meet'. Spiers then outlined very well the myth and reality of Old Firm sectarianism behaviour:

There is a richly-titillating, but utterly empty, ritual about much of the Old Firm environment today. Remarkable and unremarkable men, who have good jobs and bad and who couldn't practice bigotry if they tried, nonetheless get swept into the firmament of these occasions. Before they know it they are hollering their heads off about the Queen or the Pope or both.

Many of these people work together, drink together, play their five-a-side football in bantering friendship together, but for the Old Firm, for 90 minutes of screaming, they take choir stalls at opposite ends of the ground. Some of us who feel the fiery indignation well up within us misunderstand this aspect of contemporary Glasgow life.

Spiers mocks the English who take the Old Firm fans at their word before ridiculing the idea that there is a serious problem of violence between these fans. Having asked Strathclyde Police for the arrest figures for these 'hate-filled' encounters he found that only 24 people were arrested. These are, 'stupendously paltry statistics', he pointed out, 'for peoples supposedly needing to tear the skin off each other'. The police officer giving Spiers these statistics even pointed out that, 'A Rangers-Celtic game can sometimes be like a Sunday picnic'.

Turn the clock forward fifteen years and Graham Spiers is found at the Justice Committee debate on the Offensive Behaviour Bill supporting the criminalisation of Old Firm 'sectarian' songs. No longer prepared to tolerate (if disagree with) Billy Boys or IRA songs, Spiers asks, 'Do you want to live in a country where thousands of people can shout 'F' the Pope?'. Spiers answer was that *he* did not and that was why he was supporting the Offensive Behaviour Bill. These songs, he continued, are 'downright discrimination and prejudice' and should therefore be made illegal.[73] By 2011, Graham Spiers felt that these men who couldn't practice bigotry if they tried, who worked together and drank together, whose bantering friendship meant that violence between them was stupendously paltry, should now be arrested for the songs they sang! One can only assume that the infectious 'chattering classes' harking on about our 'hate-filled' city, backed up by journalists' vocabulary of 'hate and venom' had helped to disfigure Mr Spiers' understanding of a city's image that in the past simply 'didn't bear close scrutiny'. Back in 1996 it seems that the hype about sectarianism and violence at Old Firm games was seen as nonsense by Graham Spiers. By 2011, this 'Sunday picnic' was facing the full wrath of the state. These games had become understood as a cause of domestic violence, where the police had 'grown wearily accustomed to weeding out killers' and a poisonous milieu that shamed Scotland. With the support of Spiers, a law that could imprison these fans for up to five years for their 'sectarian' behaviour was soon to be passed.

It is worth reiterating, the rise of anti-sectarianism did not emerge because of a rise in sectarian behaviour, or of sectarian violence; yet anti-sectarianism became a significant political, media, policing and legal matter in Scotland. As we have seen, the rise of interest in sectarianism has absolutely nothing to do with the behaviour of people on the terraces or on the streets. It has, on the contrary, everything to do with the activities and rhetoric of the Scottish elites and their establishment of a virtual industry of anti-sectarianism. It appears that the 'chattering class's' moralising hatred of the Old Firm has taken centre stage.

The anti-sectarian industry

As Michael Rosie notes in *The Myth of Sectarianism*, 'Contemporary debate over perceived religious conflict is prompted by the "rebirth of Scotland"'. With constitutional change and the establishment of the Scottish Parliament, the Scots are confronted by questions of identity: Who are we? Where are we going? Where have we been?'.[74]

Rosie's insight is an important one not, simply in terms of the debate over religion, but also in terms of the development of the Scottish parliament which marked a significant shift in the political landscape of the UK. Not least, it marked the declining significance of Britishness and the Union as the unquestioned framework of political and state activity. Questions of who are we and where are we are going did indeed become relevant for the Scottish authorities at this time. It is perhaps this change to the political landscape of Scotland, more than anything else, which led to the growing interest in anti-sectarianism as an issue that could help to answer these questions.

A number of other significant shifts in political life that have influenced the rise and rise of anti-sectarianism are also worth mentioning. The first is the struggle within politics itself in the 1990s to come up with what Bill Clinton referred to as the 'big idea'. On both sides of the Atlantic, the shifting political terrain, the decline of class politics at a national level and the demise of the East/West framing of international relations helped to create a political vacuum that affected all political parties at the time. In Scotland today, for example, we are seeing a massive erosion not only of the Conservative Party but of the Labour Party too, something that would have been unimaginable a generation ago. At a time when a new type of politics was needed, anti-sectarianism, in part, became a way to fill the hole at the heart of politics, something that appeared to offer both substance and a sense of purpose.

The second shift involves the rise of the 'politics of behaviour', encompassing the development of a whole array of new features on the political terrain including ASBOs, smoking bans, health awareness campaigns and 'nudge' initiatives (seen most recently with the SNP's increased price of alcohol and their attempt to *make* us all responsible drinkers). For governments both north and south of the border, micro-managing the behaviour of the population has become the new guiding objective. As John Flint has observed, there has been something of an interrelationship between antisocial behaviour policies and anti-sectarianism, with governments increasingly becoming involved in the day-to-day lives of people in an attempt to regulate the conduct of citizens and to make them fit a new model of civility.

As we have seen, campaigning around anti-sectarianism began in earnest at the end of the 1990s, helped by the formation of *Nil by Mouth* in 1999. Here we witnessed another interesting trend emerge, a victim campaign group developing out of a personal tragedy. This type of campaigning first occurred in the UK in 1990 when the first 'Mothers Against...' initiatives developed. It was something that had occurred in the USA ten years earlier with campaigns like 'Mothers Against Drink Driving'. Again, what appears to reflect a new form of victim identity and individual form of campaigning came about in the UK at exactly the same time as collective political and social forms of self identification declined. Most crucially, this development helped to create a new point of connection for politicians who increasingly began to rally around individuals, groups and forms of identification that took as their starting point their victim status. One of the recent outcomes of this within the Criminal Justice System is the emphasis placed upon 'victim justice', a development that was of some relevance to the Offensive Behaviour Bill.

The vicious murder of Mark Scott helped trigger some of the campaigning around anti-sectarianism, but it was the wider political and social trends that resulted in the anti-sectarianism industry forming at this time. As such, the outlook of Cara Henderson, a middle-class young woman who had never been to an Old Firm game before and saw 'killers' when she looked at Old Firm fans, was happily supported and incorporated into the framework of anti-sectarianism and the most extreme cases of violence became a benchmark for understanding the apparent sectarian mindset of Old Firm fans.[75] Within politics, MSP Donald Gorrie pushed for new anti-sectarian laws, and by 2002 the Labour leader and First Minister Jack McConnell started his own campaign against *sectarianism in Scotland*. Sectarianism now became 'Scotland's Shame'.

Discussing his own proposed laws to tackle sectarianism, First Minister McConnell explained that, 'These measures signal our determination that Scotland will no longer tolerate acts of religious hatred. We will act to toughen the law so that courts can more severely punish crimes motivated by sectarianism' (*Guardian* 5th December 2002). When launching the report of the Cross Party Working Group on Religious Hatred, he explained, 'I want Scotland to be a society where we respect cultural differences and celebrate our rich and diverse religious traditions. I want all Scots to be proud of the Scotland we live in today'. Portraying the intolerance of sectarian Scots as a problem for the nation, McConnell added:

> We need to put sectarianism in the dust-bin of history. Scotland must play a full part in Europe and the global economy, so we cannot allow ourselves to be dragged down by the deadweight of religious hatred and sectarian bigotry.[76]

Sectarianism became seen as a problem for the image of Scotland, a problem associated with violence that threatened the role Scotland could play in Europe and endangered national economic development. Once anti-sectarianism was highlighted as an important campaigning issue for politicians, it became important to emphasise the seriousness of this problem. In many ways, Graham Spiers warning about the chattering classes 'harking on about this "hate-filled" city of ours' had come true. Except now these petty prejudices had moved out of the wine bars and into the chamber of the Scottish parliament. As anti-sectarianism became institutionalised and turned into an unquestioned and unquestionable political and moral good, exaggerating the problem became the done thing. The 'great strides' mentioned by Spiers 'in softening the divide' were now forgotten or ignored, while the 'utterly empty ritual' carried out at Old Firm games by men who 'couldn't practice bigotry if they tried' now became reinterpreted as a serious problem of religious intolerance. This would, so the argument went, lead to violence on the streets and was a pressing matter needing education, policing, and new laws; a problem that was holding Scotland back from playing its 'full part in Europe and the global economy'.

The 2002 Scottish bid to joint host the European Championships with Ireland in 2008 no doubt helped to encourage McConnell to play the anti-sectarian card as a way of showing they were a government and nation who could be taken seriously by the cosmopolitan elites of Europe. Indeed, Europe in the guise of UEFA subsequently played a critical role in pushing the Scottish government further still in their policing of offensiveness in football.

An anti-sectarian industry began to grow prominently at this time, with grants being awarded to beat bigotry. Discussions started in 2001 between Celtic and Rangers about their possible involvement in the new ministerial group to tackle sectarianism. The campaign Sense over Sectarianism was launched; the public-sector trade union Unison came out in opposition to sectarianism; even former James Bond star Sean Connery came forward to oppose bigotry. Football club-based campaigns like Bhoys Against Bigotry were set up and the National Union of Students in Scotland created their own anti-sectarianism campaign. By 2006, an Action Plan on Sectarianism was set up by the Scottish Government with the aim of creating a tolerant and 'truly multicultural and multi-faith Scotland'. Teaching tolerance, with reference to sectarianism, consequently became part and parcel of children's education in Scotland.

Initiative followed initiative, incorporating councils, schools, football teams, the SFA, the Scottish Government, youth groups and the police in the 'fight against bigotry'. A National Club Licensing Scheme was even introduced making it a necessity for Scottish football league clubs to show evidence of their policies to fight racism and sectarianism in football. And, in 2006, the Scottish Executive launched Calling Full Time on Sectarianism, a government initiative set up to challenge misbehaviour and abusive chanting, something that it declared was:

Harmful to Scottish football and can present a very negative image of Scottish society, both domestically and across the world. This situation must be addressed if we are to secure a bright future for Scotland where bigotry, intolerance and hatred do not exist and where sectarianism is consigned to history.[77]

With all of this in mind, the statement in 2011 by Roseanna Cunningham that, 'You can either do nothing and allow the status quo... or we can take the strong action needed now and send out a message loud and clear that this behaviour is not going to be tolerated any longer', seems all the more ridiculous. By 2006, Scottish society and institutions were already riddled with anti-sectarian programmes; anti-sectarianism (rather than sectarianism) was at the very heart of Scottish political life. For Old Firm fans in particular, listening to the rhetoric surrounding the Offensive Behaviour Bill, it must have seemed like Groundhog Day. However, this time it was the newly-elected majority SNP government and the First Minister Alex Salmond who stood at the pulpit of tolerance and denounced the sectarian hordes.

Tolerant Scotland
Professor John Flint has described the various anti-sectarian activities as the 'most intensive and sustained focus on governing sectarianism in the post-Second World War period'.[78] He is right. However, this is not simply about sectarianism, but rather, sectarianism fits into the wider and more important development of 'tolerance' as a governing framework: anti-sectarian politics, journalists, initiatives, campaigns, education, awareness, training, policing, groups and laws all act as a flagship of tolerance in Scotland.

Being 'tolerant' is the badge you must now wear if you are going to be successful in politics, or in any key institution in Scotland. It has become an unquestioned good, and politicians fall over themselves to claim the tolerance mantle. During the final parliamentary debate on the Offensive Behaviour Act, time and again MSPs would stand up and explain that they were 'against bigotry of any kind'. As speaker after speaker got up to repeat this scripted line, it became increasingly clear that this was not a political idea or belief, but a mantra, a chant. It allowed those opposed to the bill to show their respects, doff their cap at the altar of anti-racism and anti-sectarianism – assured of the murmured concurring of their opponents – and then make their points. All these speakers, if asked, would automatically describe themselves as 'tolerant'. But today tolerance means something very different from the original idea which constituted the foundation of the defence of free speech. Now tolerance means respecting difference; it also embodies a therapeutic dimension, one that recognises that words hurt, and one that demands respect for people's identities. Given this, you can already see the problem that exists for football fans who are often offensive to one another. Respecting difference is not usually the first thing on a supporters mind as they unfurl their banners and take on the local rivals.

For over a decade, the promotion of tolerance has become an essential aspect of being part of the new Scottish establishment. The answer to Rosie's question, 'Who are we?' is that we are a 'modern tolerant Scotland'. Since 1997, for example, not only in politics, but in religion as well, tolerance, and showing that you are tolerant has become essential. The Church of Scotland argued back then that there was 'no time for intolerance' within the church, and that the church must, 'tackle Orange Order bigotry' (Herald 30th September 1998). This was later followed by the Catholic Church defensively arguing that, 'We're all for tolerance', when they were put under pressure about their position on shared school campuses (Herald 28th January 2004). From the start of the new millennium new expressions of tolerance developed, most noticeably with the One Scotland, Many Cultures government advertising and awareness campaign. Here, another key framework of 'tolerance' – anti-racism – was promoted across Scotland. Initially planned as a short awareness-raising campaign, the Many Cultures promotion lasted for many years and is still in play today. Illustrative of the disconnected nature of politics, the development of this initiative and the slogan itself came not from a social movement or even from leaders of key institutions in society, but from a focus group and an advertising agency.

The buzzword 'tolerance' was accompanied by 'respect' and 'awareness', the correct form of behaviour being to 'accept others', to be multicultural and to be non-judgemental. This norm of tolerance explains why the Scottish police began to see themselves as a force for 'Celebrating and Valuing Difference' and why ACPOS produced their own Equality & Diversity Strategy.

The tolerance badge was stamped not only upon the issue of racism and sectarianism, but also related to other so called 'vulnerable groups'. The laws that we have looked at so far, in terms of racial, religious and also offensive behaviour, all fit within the rubric of tolerance and the perceived need to create a tolerant Scotland. For the Offensive Behaviour Bill, the need for tolerance meant the defence of gay, transgender and disabled people, for example. The intolerant behaviour of football fans, in all these respects, would no longer be acceptable in Scotland. Fan groups themselves, even the 'ultra' Rangers fan groups, have felt the need to show that they too are tolerant. Following a protest against the Offensive Behaviour Bill, a statement was released explaining why they were protesting but also (defensively) pointing out that, 'The Union Bears and The Blue Order would like to make it clear we are against sectarianism and racism in all forms'.

Anti-sectarianism, was part of a wider development of tolerance-based ideas, attitudes and politics, but as a specifically Scottish phenomenon it also provided something unique for the new elites to get their teeth into – their own platform for demonstrating their particularly tolerant nature. By 2006, the Scottish Executive explained that: 'Tackling sectarianism in football is central to creating the truly multi-cultural and multi-faith Scotland that people aspire to and deserve – a Scotland where difference is the basis for mutual respect and understanding'.[79]

In this respect, the call for tolerance appears to be entirely positive and unproblematic. However, there are difficulties with this approach. For example, multiculturalism risks relativising beliefs and leaching out any meaning from values. Trevor Philips, the chairman of the Commission for Racial Equality, has raised his own concerns that multicultural policies risk segregating communities along ethnic lines and actually prevent ethnic minorities from becoming fully integrated into British society. This is perhaps the main reason why the One Scotland, Many Cultures slogan was quietly dropped and replaced simply with One Scotland.

Similarly, in religion, the attempt to become tolerant runs the risk of emptying out traditional values from religious doctrines. The Church of Scotland in 2011 published a document, Scotland many cultures: a study guide for Christians, where in the first section, Knowing me, knowing you, notes are provided to 'explore...the importance of churches to local life'. It is immediately interesting that, like an inclusive youth group, the leader of this 'many cultures' workshop does not explain but 'explores' – he does not lead, but facilitates. And facilitates what? Not a discussion about the importance of the Church of Scotland, but of all churches. Are all churches equally valid? If so why join the Church of Scotland? Why indeed should the Church of Scotland actually exist?

As Christianity is recast as a form of cultural inclusion and a form of 'participation', the intolerance of some church goers to issues like gay marriage or gay ministers often end up embarrassing liberal church leaders who feel the need to modernise and, consequently, relativise. The homophobia of African bishops may make the Archbishop of Canterbury choke on his soup, but all they are doing is standing up for what were, until relatively recently, fairly basic Christian values. It is almost getting to the stage where you can be a Christian without actually believing in God. In consequence, part and parcel of the new tolerance framework appears to be a repulsion of strong beliefs or absolute values. The only absolute, in a sense, is that of tolerance. But tolerance itself is not a value.

Tolerance old and new
Historically, tolerance was not about limiting free speech so as to protect the sensibilities of different groups in society. It was the very opposite of this, representing a rejection of state power over control of speech and behaviour and a belief that people's ideas, however repellent, should be tolerated.

The promotion of tolerance developed with John Locke and later with John Stuart Mill. The development of this notion of tolerance was partly pragmatic but also related to a principled defence of freedom of conscience, belief, and later on, behaviour. For Mill, the measure of tolerance was the extent to which people could think, speak and behave freely without restraints and interference from the state. The trenchant belief in freedom of speech was not predicated on a sense that simply 'anything goes', or that 'everyone's opinions and behaviour are equally valid'. On the contrary, tolerating free speech was coupled with the equally important belief that ideas and behaviour could and should be judged and challenged. Freedom to believe was permitted but this did not mean respect had to be given to these beliefs (or 'cultures') themselves. We were all free to challenge and even ridicule one another's words and deeds. The notion of tolerance was a liberating starting point for intellectual and moral contestation, development and improvement: Within a tolerant society, ideas and ways of behaving could be challenged, the truth sought and a more civilised society nurtured.

To tolerate something, one first had to judge it, disagree with it but also accept that it should not be controlled by the authorities simply because one thought it was wrong or repugnant. You do not have to *tolerate* ideas that you agree with. You tolerate wrong ideas and behaviour but also challenge these reactionary viewpoints and actions. For Mill, the principle was clear – as long as no physical or economic harm was done to an individual, ideas and behaviour should be tolerated – even, and indeed especially, ideas that you found abhorrent or upsetting. 'Wrong' ideas or behaviour were useful for Mill because they continually encouraged society to challenge them, thus strengthening the understanding of ideas across the populace. This was important not only for the free development of ideas and beliefs but also, and equally, for the development of individual moral autonomy. He who lets the world choose his plan of life for him, Mill argued, has no need of any other ability than that of imitation. But this is not the action of a man; it is merely the action of an ape. Part of the belief in the importance of personal moral development came from an idea that it was wrong to force beliefs onto people. The goal was to encourage a vibrant culture made up of autonomous individuals who were free to think and act and also to challenge one another's behaviour. For the German philosopher Immanuel Kant, respect was given to people and their freedoms as part of a belief that this would help encourage the development of reason and conduct which genuinely belonged to each individual. Everyone was to become judgemental, to make their own judgements and decisions, and to take responsibility for their own actions.

Incorrect or wrong choices were not centrally important for Mill. More crucial was what manner of men and women it was that were acting in the first place; what type of individual was making the choice. In a sense, as Furedi notes in *On Tolerance*, Mill wanted everybody to be a heretic – to be a free choosing man – rather than a sheep, repeating the latest correct and inoffensive mantra. Tolerance was difficult. Accepting rather than punishing those whose views and behaviour you hated required strength and maturity, and most of all a belief in the importance of freedom. As George Orwell noted, if democracy means anything it is the right to tell people what they do not want to hear.[80] We retain our dignity, Furedi argues, only by insisting that no official can withhold an opinion from us. Likewise, we only become robust human beings by being faced with conflict, by encountering difficult and even offensive ideas and forms of behaviour. Words may well hurt, but dealing with them can develop individual character, a more vibrant public life and a more articulate society.[81]

Today, in comparison, the meaning of tolerance has been transformed. This has developed over many decades across the Western world, Furedi notes, with little discussion or clarification about what this thing *tolerance* now actually means. Tolerance means the opposite of what it used to. It is now about being non-judgemental, about limiting hurtful speech and behaviour, about increasing state power to protect the people who are seen as fragile and vulnerable. It has become a personal characteristic, a badge of decency, disconnected from the idea of freedom or even thought. It has also become about 'respecting difference': not respecting individual freedoms as such, but 'respecting' statically-defined groups and identities. It has also become a form of politeness based on an understanding that these groups and identities are easily bruised by things we say, beliefs we have and types of behaviour we exhibit. Consequently, having offensive ideas or behaving in an offensive way is understood to cause alarm or distress and needs to be regulated or made illegal. Rather than tolerance being about individual freedom and the autonomy of individuals being respected, it has become about respecting groups and group identities and protecting them from harm.

At a time when it appears that tolerance is all the rage, the reality is we live in profoundly intolerant times. This is why the notion of zero tolerance and a plethora of zero-tolerance policies and initiatives have developed over the last two decades at the same time as politicians talk endlessly about the need for tolerance. 'Tolerance' becomes a state-enforced form of behaviour – the very opposite of its original meaning – a formulaic etiquette that does not require you to think, but merely to show respect.

One of the many unintended consequences of this is that at the very same time that anti-sectarianism and anti-racism are relentlessly promoted, they lose any weight or depth of meaning – they become empty. Being against racism and sectarianism in all its forms has become a mantra, disconnected from ideas or from real practice. The students that I teach, for example, almost all claim to be against racism in all its forms, but have very different and indeed conflicting views about how we should relate to and treat immigrants. For them, as for the rest of society, being against racism and sectarianism is simply about being polite, not being offensive, not calling people names that might be hurtful. As Žižek comments above, it is about respecting the other's right not to be 'harassed'.

In an attempt to understand the impact of their anti-racist *One Scotland, Many Cultures* campaign in 2005, the Scottish Government asked the research group System 3 to talk to the public. To judge the success of this tolerance initiative, System 3 attempted to discover whether or not Scottish people thought using the term Paki or Chinky was 'seriously racist'. Other similar questions were asked about the politeness of Scots to different ethnic groups because anti-racism was largely assessed in terms of the correct language being used, the awareness of the public about their language and, especially, their sensitivity to the potentially hurtful nature of certain words. In many respects, the benchmark for being a good tolerant anti-racist was whether or not you had adopted the correct, emotionally-sensitive etiquette. This is what being an anti-racist means under the rules of the new tolerant elite.[82] New tolerant anti-racism is a performance, it is nothing to do with what type of person you are, very little to do with your beliefs, and very much to do with your unthinking deployment of the correct terminology and proscribed codes of behaviour.

Governing through intolerant tolerance

The changing meaning of tolerance has been focused upon here because it is one of the central reasons why anti-sectarianism became such a useful resource for the Scottish authorities in the new century. Tolerance had come to mean 'respecting difference'; it is a form of emotional correctness, an awareness of the sensitivity of others, of the potential hurtfulness of words. Over time, the engagement with this new form of tolerance has increasingly led to words being criminalised. By 2012, with the passing of the Offensive Behaviour Act, offensiveness itself was made into a policing matter. To be tolerant now meant arresting fans for uttering offensive words.

Discussing the new football bill, Roseanna Cunningham would repeat time and again that bigoted ideas or behaviour were not acceptable in a 'tolerant Scotland'. In Scottish schools children are now taught the importance of 'respecting difference', while football clubs in Scotland must prove that they are institutionalising anti-sectarian awareness initiatives. 'Respecting difference' is understood and represented as a morally important standpoint. However, despite representation to the contrary, there is nothing substantively moral or progressive about 'respecting difference'. As Furedi argues, 'diversity' has become truly elevated to a moral virtue. But why, he asks, is a mere fact of life, difference, better than similitude? What are the values of 'difference' or 'diversity' other than the representation of things that are not the same?

For Frank Furedi, the reason that elites have adopted this new tolerance framework is because they are unclear about what they stand for today. The new tolerance is a pragmatic defence of valueless values: What do you stand for? I stand for difference! Few elites, Furedi notes, can give meaning to national unity today. What unites people is unclear; even talking about national unity is difficult. What is it that can encourage minorities to assimilate, what binds people together? What is the common good that we can agree upon and organise society around?

> Instead of elaborating a public ethos that can guide and inspire a community, people are exhorted to celebrate diversity...Through the sacralisation of diversity...a divided society is miraculously reborn as a diverse one, and tolerance is called upon to respect and celebrate it (Furedi 2011: 71).

For a newly-developing Scottish elite with few of the traditional political points of reference to guide their developing institutions in the twenty-first century, new tolerance, and consequently, anti-sectarianism, became a necessary crutch to lean upon.

There are no real values being promoted with all this anti-sectarian campaigning; no political or religious ideas referred to. Rather, the issue is constantly discussed in terms of how you 'behave' – did you cause offense? 'Fenian blood' or IRA songs are not being challenged for religious or political reasons, but because they are deemed hurtful. Consequently, the state is able to carve out a new role for itself, connecting with our sense of vulnerability and policing the language of the intolerant. Anti-sectarianism, and the myriad anti-sectarian initiatives in schools, youth clubs, sports centres, football clubs and even in the Scottish Parliament are, in many respects, a form of anti-bullying awareness training. Through this therapeutic prism, certain words are treated like weapons, as profoundly damaging and traumatising. Consequently, classical notions of freedom of speech become a problem; indeed, in the guise of offensive football fans, free speech becomes criminalised.

However, not too long ago the idea of tolerance meant something very different: it meant you tolerated other people's ideas, beliefs and words. Children were taught that sticks and stones did not break bones and individuals were expected to recognise the difference between words and actions. Words and their free use were considered important in a free society; name-calling might make children cry, but adults would teach them to deal with this and to grow up.

As Furedi argues, tolerance has come to mean being non-judgemental; it means we should not challenge or question or offend different 'cultures' in any way. To judge is now to be hurtful and we must unthinkingly offer respect towards 'difference' and 'diversity'. Being tolerant is not about being free, it is simply the done thing. As such, the state and politicians in Scotland can stretch their hands across myriad real and imaginary barricades and give affirmation to a variety of groups in society. 'We respect you', they say, 'and will not accept intolerant behaviour in any form'.

Today's tolerance closes down debate (and even thought) because of the perceived danger of offending different groups. More than this, the high moral ground given to tolerance means that intolerance becomes understood as the cause of serious conflicts in society. In the UNESCO Declaration on Tolerance, a whole range of activities are seen to flow from intolerance, including violence, terrorism, aggressive nationalism, marginalisation of vulnerable groups, intimidation and so on. All of these can, 'threaten the consolidation of peace and democracy, both nationally and internationally, and are obstacles to development'.[83] In this childlike worldview, the economic, social and political tensions that influence violence and conflict in society disappear and we are left with nothing more than the 'dangers of intolerance'.

This myopic view of 'intolerance equals violence' is one of the reasons
sectarianism is seen as such a problem today. Intolerant sectarian name-calling
becomes a profound issue, in part, because it is seamlessly connected to brutal
acts of violence and even murder. Intolerance on one issue is assumed to mean
intolerance on everything. As a result, in the imagination of the 'tolerant
elite', the Rangers man screaming 'up to our knees in Fenian blood' is assumed
not only to be viciously sectarian but also a racist, a homophobe and a wife
beater as well. The discussion about sectarianism in Scotland interconnects
all sorts of disparate issues, stretching from offensive football fans, to urban
disorder, gangs on estates, domestic violence, drunkenness, knife crime and so
on. In the end, the term sectarian itself becomes synonymous with violence;
especially working-class violence. To oppose sectarianism is to oppose violence,
being anti-sectarian means standing up for victims of crime.

Conclusion

The behaviour of football fans has nothing to do with free speech in the classical
sense. People are not speaking to one another at a game, they are shouting
at one another. You do not have a discussion or a contestation of ideas; you
generally just hurl insults and shout each other down. This is not a 'free speech
situation'. However, the criminalisation of football fans is a serious restriction
upon the freedom of expression and behaviour. This is a form of expression that
many people may disapprove of, but historically in a liberal society, disapproval
did not lead to arrests and imprisonment.

The new intolerant tolerance jars with those accustomed to heated banter.
Having talked to old football fans at Ibrox, many simply don't understand
the problem. Why on Earth would shouting stuff at a football game become a
big deal or a political problem? 'Water off a duck's back', they say, shrug their
shoulders and look puzzled. However, the idea of being able to ignore offensive
comments or songs as 'water off a duck's back' is no longer the appropriate
moral standpoint. Showing your outrage at intolerance and showing that you
are offended becomes a 'good'. To be thin-skinned, to complain to the police,
to be shocked and outraged become part and parcel of the correct form of
behaviour.

The new moralising form of tolerance has become a central framework
around which the new Scottish elite and its institutions have organised
themselves. As such, nobody has an interest in denying the problem of
sectarianism; indeed, the opposite is the case. Even the Protestant Kirk is
happy to exaggerate the problem and to apologise for anything it did in the past
that was sectarian, thus cleansing itself and entering the tolerant fold of the
new elite. To be a 'right-thinking person' in Scotland today you must be and be
seen to be tolerant.

The American social thinker Russell Jacoby, describing a similar obsession
with tolerance in the United States, noted that, 'Liberals and leftists run the

show. They define themselves by their enthusiasm for multiculturalism – the more you support it, the more virtuous you are'.[84] For these liberals and leftists, challenging the notion of tolerance and multiculturalism was like 'questioning recycling'. Stripped of any singular vision, progress is reformulated around the 'celebration of diversity'. Without a coherent sense of culture, incoherence is magically turned into a positive attribute through the promotion of 'many cultures'. Regarding the new Scottish elites' and their embrace of tolerance, Jacoby's insight about the collapse of leadership and ideas is telling:

> Stripped of its radical idiom, robbed of its utopian hope, liberals and leftists retreat in the name of progress to celebrate diversity. With few ideas on how a future should be shaped, they embrace all ideas. Pluralism becomes the catch-all, the alpha and omega of political thinking. Dressed up in multiculturalism, it has become the opium of disillusioned intellectuals, the ideology of an era without an ideology.[85]

More recently, in his new book *Coming Apart: The State of White America*, the conservative Charles Murray has observed that the American upper classes no longer preach to the masses about what is right and wrong. They are a hollow elite, he argues, who have given up and prefer instead to preach 'non-judgementalism'.[86] In our case, here, the fig leaf of 'tolerance' is an abdication of leadership, a form of political pragmatism for an elite that finds it difficult to inspire the public, develop a sense of commonality or to give meaning to national unity.

The modern meaning of tolerance also gives the authorities a new framework for regulating a public they are out of touch with and nervous about. Appealing to radicals and liberals over past issues associated with oppression, anti-racism and anti-sectarianism become merely matters of law, policing and the criminalisation of speech. Following the United States, Scotland's valorisation of modern day tolerance has led to the creation of 'hate crimes' and the increasing arrest and imprisonment of the poorest sections of society who have not been to the new elite's finishing schools.

Today's bizarre concern about football fans singing songs and waving flags, the ridiculous talk about religious hate crime, and the impassioned language of offence have nothing to do with sectarianism or with violent activities of Old Firm fans. But they do have a lot to do with the elite and the middle class's pressing need for a moral crutch of 'tolerance'. At least with anti-racist policies there was a real issue with racial inequality that gave at least some meaning to new regulations. The further irony with anti-sectarianism is that there are no real differences in the lives of Catholics and Protestants in Scotland. 'Sectarianism' is kept alive as an issue not by the 'hate-filled bigots' at football grounds, but by the new tolerant elite's desperation to hold onto an issue that gives them a sense of goodness and apparent moral purpose.

Each time a 'new' and 'modern' Scotland is proclaimed, the pantomime villain of sectarianism is held aloft by the first minister who can stand tall, looking enlightened and morally resolute. Despite difficulties in answering questions about where Scotland is going, or even what Scottish independence actually means, politicians can always rely upon the unquestioned mantra of opposing 'racism and sectarianism in all its forms'.

This reliance on anti-sectarianism and the badge of tolerance reflects an unsureness of belief and purpose in the elite and it is this lack of certainty, meaning and direction to political and public life which constantly leads to both a sense of anxiety amongst the elites and a desire to regulate the words and behaviour of the public. The time and energy spent on attempting to 'send out the message' that sectarianism is 'unacceptable' (at a time when almost everyone in Scotland agrees that it is unacceptable) suggests a genuine level of fear and even paranoia about the disconnected elites' view of the plebs who watch football matches. In their worst moments, the Scottish authorities appear to operate under the principle that if they do not do more to stem the tide of sectarianism the streets will be filled with flaming torches and screaming mobs. This is a problem inside the empty heads and hearts of the elite itself rather than a real problem in Scottish society.

7

Conclusion: Challenging Cosmopolitan Myths: 'Man Up'

One person with a belief is equal to a force of 99 who have only interests.

J.S. MILL, *REPRESENTATIVE GOVERNMENT*

I BEGAN THIS BOOK BY THINKING ABOUT HOW THE CRIMINALISATION OF FOOTBALL fans had changed over time and used the Hillsborough disaster as one of the clearest examples of old-style authoritarian policing. At this time, fans were depicted as a mob, part of the alien enemy within, and caged like animals. Today, as we have seen, the criminalisation of fans, in the Hillsborough sense, has been transformed. For example, in May 2012, a newspaper article was headlined, 'Police probe web page that mocked fans tragedy' (*Scotsman* 8th May 2012). The article revealed that a Facebook page mocking the Hillsborough tragedy had been created; following complaints to the police, the matter was investigated which led to Facebook taking down the page. Now, rather than physically cage fans into grounds, the role of the police is to wrap us in cotton wool and protect us from offensive words; today's therapeutic police force polices hurt feelings. In this latter Hillsborough case, a police spokesman proudly explained that the investigation was being carried out by the CID and, 'Detectives from the force's hi-tech crime unit'. Elsewhere, in April 2012, the comedian Alan Davies was being dragged over the coals and faced a twitter storm for daring to suggest that it was ridiculous for Liverpool to refuse to play a match simply because it was the anniversary of Hillsborough. But as one columnist noted, 'Hillsborough is now surrounded by a force field of emotional correctness'. Davies tried to stand by the point he was making, that we all suffer tragedy but life must go on; nevertheless, he also felt the need, indeed the moral pressure, to apologise and make a donation to the Hillsborough campaign.

If you had suggested to fans in 1989 that this was how things would turn out, they would have laughed. The idea that the role of the police would be to protect fans from offensive comments was, until relatively recently, unimaginable. Moreover, if you had suggested that fans themselves would be telling tales on one another because of these comments, you would not have been taken seriously again. But times have changed. Today, the policing of offensiveness is the key issue when looking at the criminalisation of fans. If anything, it is more reactionary and dangerous than the bullyboy antics of the police in the 1980s because it is a direct attack on people's behaviour, words, even their thoughts – something that Stephen Birrell and many others are finding out.

Cosmopolitan myths
In Scotland, the case for stopping offensive behaviour at football is bound up with the notion of progress, of being more civilised, more caring and so on. It is also bound up with the notion that it is the educated, the self-aware and the rational who are attempting to do something about the less educated, the backward and prejudiced. However, as we have seen in Scotland, across the UK and even in Europe, the reality is very different; whatever the prejudices of the mass of fans, the myths perpetuated about these fans highlight a serious problem about the elite themselves.

Fans across the UK are understood to be racist or, at the very least, in need of constant race-awareness training. In Scotland, it is sectarianism that needs never-ending summits, laws, charities and initiatives to counter this supposed problem. Yet the arrests at games for racist behaviour for the last fifteen years has been incredibly small, while sectarian-related arrests at football are low, often relating to words shouted at the police. Where individual court cases of 'sectarian' fans shouting at grounds come to light, it is rare to see the caricatured hate-filled bigot. Instead, we are left with cases of young men who are apologetic, embarrassed and frequently devastated by the experience of being arrested and, at times, losing their jobs.

Fans across the UK cannot be trusted. They act like 'Pavlov's foaming dogs' one columnist informs us, and yet the violence carried out by these suggestible animals appears to be small, less than in the past and far less than levels in other European countries (*Evening Standard* 27th January 2012). The policing of violence is a more targeted part of police activities at games today. However, there remains an underlying presumption that fans are volatile and their behaviour and chants need to be closely monitored and limited. Football games, especially big games with tens of thousands of supporters are not tea parties exactly, but as Mark Dingwall from the Rangers Trust has pointed out, there is less than one arrest that leads to a conviction for every game at Ibrox – violence at games is the exception not the rule.

Further afield, in Europe, we have seen how the myth of the sex slave abusing football fan was falsely formulated during the Germany World Cup Finals in 2006. Television adverts, increased border policing, government helplines, even concern expressed by the President of the United States, resulted from the concern about trafficked prostitutes. This again turned out to be a total fiction built on the hate filled fantasies of both the old conservative and new cosmopolitan elites.

As Euro 2012 kicked off, the question of racism and even fascism hits the headlines. Will English fans be safe in the Ukraine? Should players walk off the pitch if they are abused in Poland? Should UEFA officials resign if there is any sign of racism at the grounds? Questions are even being asked about whether the competition should ever have been given to countries that are clearly not as tolerant and enlightened as us Brits. Johnny Foreigner is still inferior it seems, but now it's because he hasn't been to one of our anti-racism finishing schools. Don't go to the Euros, Sol Campbell tells us in the hysterical BBC *Panorama* documentary entitled 'Stadiums of Hate', or you could 'come back in a coffin'.

As I finish writing this book, Euro 2012 is being played and yet the army of Polish and Ukrainian racist/fascist killers have yet to materialise. In fact, as Tim Black has usefully pointed out, even some of the people who appeared on the 'Stadiums of Hate' programme have come out and condemned this one-sided representation of 'bastions of intolerance'. In a letter to the *Economist*, Jonathan Ornstein, the director of the Jewish Community Centre of Krakow, protested the 'unethical' nature of the documentary. All the contrary opinions expressed to the *Panorama* journalist, Ornstein explains, were omitted. Black and Jewish footballers who enjoyed their time in Poland were not given air-time so that the one-sided message of bigotry and danger could be put forward. Rather than Poland being a place of profound reaction and danger for anyone, especially ethnic minorities, travelling to the Euros, Ornstein tells Tim Black, 'I would say that, as a Jew walking around Krakow, wearing a Kippur, I think you're just about safer here than you are anywhere in Western Europe'.[87] Again, a phenomenally biased and malevolent representation of football fans is produced – a fiction presented and consumed by the 'enlightened' and 'tolerant' British cosmopolitan elites.

Regardless of the facts, the myth of the uneducated, prejudice filled, bigoted and abusive fan, passes from one panic to the next. In Scotland, this has helped to construct new categories of offence, like 'Old Firm domestic violence', and once again the perfect knuckle dragging abusive bogey man is conjured up by those in authority. Brutal, extreme and unusual murders are given political meaning and significance, while talk of 'killing fields' at Old Firm games is taken as a reflection of reality; bad misrepresentations fuel the talk of 'shame' and outrage about 'religious hate crime', with few if any questions raised about the false image of the 'sectarian problem at the heart of Scotland'. Oddly, despite an anti-sectarian industry having grown exponentially over the last decade, the current SNP government can, in all seriousness, hold forth and act as if little has been done to 'do something' about the problems in Scottish football.

My own experience of campaigning against the Offensive Behaviour Bill was illuminating, not least in terms of how such a serious piece of legislation could be discussed in an often unserious way. As long as you are denouncing sectarianism it appears, anything goes. On a Radio Scotland debate programme with myself and the SNP's Humza Yousaf, the MSP explained that after an Old Firm game his cousin was asked if he was a Catholic or a Protestant. Yousaf's Asian cousin (apparently) replied, 'No I am a Muslim', to which the inquisitor asked, 'Yes, but are you a Catholic Muslim or a Protestant Muslim?'. Discussing this fable with Celtic and Rangers fans afterwards, the point was made by both that this was in fact an old old joke that had been told in Glasgow and Belfast for decades. One particularly irate Rangers fan, 'Mitch', emailed me after the show to complain about what he saw as the MSPs 'lies'. It read:

BY FAR, *the worst offender was* MSP *Humza Yousaf with his blatant lies! I actually emailed him to pull him up about this (I get the impression I wasn't alone!) and, like any "good" politician, he is trying to wriggle out of it and backtrack – clearly he is not familiar with the "listen again" feature which lets us hear exactly what he said!*

Another point of interest was that it was often those on the left of politics who held the most negative views about working-class football fans. Consequently, the people who in the past fought against moral panics are often supportive of new authoritarian forms of policing and surveillance. Discussing the bill with an old Marxist, for instance, he used the example of 1930s Germany to explain why laws like the Offensive Behaviour Bill should be supported – as if Scotland today could be compared to Germany and the rise of fascism eighty years ago. Let these crazy fans sing their bigoted songs and in no time there'll be lines of goose-stepping mobs marching down Sauchiehall Street! Similarly, on Radio Four's *Moral Maze*, it was another man of the 'left', the ex-advisor to Tony Blair, Matthew Taylor, who was the most reactionary on the subject of Old Firm fans. For Taylor, there was a direct connection between songs sung at games and the murder of Celtic fans. He explained that he believed in a 'broken windows' theory regarding this issue – in other words he saw fans as a monkey-see, monkey-do (or perhaps more accurately monkey-hear, monkey-do) mob, riled up at games before they hit the killing fields once again.[88] Taylor is now head of the highly respected and respectable RSA and writes about the need for a 'new Enlightenment'. He is an archetypal member of the new elite, a member of the most intolerant group in society.

I have made the point already, but it is worth restating that if any of the above prejudices, exaggerations, myths or lies had been made about a minority group or one seen as being discriminated against, there would be outrage in society – and rightly so. However, as we have seen in the writings of journalists like Graham Spiers, times change, the nature of the elite changes and, consequently, prejudices in society change. To be 'radical' or 'enlightened' today means supporting the criminalisation of behaviour and words, especially when muttered by working-class football fans. To be a modern day tolerant individual you must be passionately intolerant of certain views and opinions; you must be what was once called an authoritarian.

Hatred and prejudice may exist in football, but some kinds of hatred are more acceptable than others. In reality, the prejudices of the 'right-thinking people' compete with and often outdo those of fans. Exaggerations, falsehoods, myths and even name calling are typically used in public and political discussions about football supporters. Accompanying these prejudices, the policing and regulation of supporters has escalated relentlessly over the last few decades. Today, grounds are filling up with police officers armed with the latest mobile cameras and listening equipment, creating, in the process, a level of surveillance more suited to an apocalyptic science-fiction film than an afternoon of entertainment.

Immature elite

When studying problems associated with the Old Firm, the focus for public and academic study alike is usually 'the problem of sectarianism'. In this book, I have attempted to turn this around and suggest the way to understand problems associated with the Old Firm, and the way to understand the issue of sectarianism, is to look at the rise of anti-sectarianism as a force in society. Instead of looking down our noses at the people 'on the terraces', we should raise our gaze a little and take a long hard look at the new elites. This is important because the new trends in society – the new prejudices, myths and beliefs – tend to come from people, organisations and institutions that wield power rather than from the man on the street.

Looking at the Offensive Behaviour Act, and the political storm created during its promotion, is interesting as a way of looking at the elites, and in particular the political elite in Scotland today. The casual use of 'facts' and statistics which overlapped with rhetoric and distortions was a common feature of the campaign that promoted the bill. Some MSPS appeared to be unserious in their attempt to look at the myths and reality of the problems they were addressing. This however is not simply a shortcoming in the character of MSPS but rather reflects a general immaturity within the authorities. Before a new law with such significant powers as the Offensive Behaviour Act is even considered, one would expect our rulers to do their homework, to consider the existing legislation and to formulate a coherent bill. None of this was apparent when the law was first promoted and much criticism was made of the incoherent and shabby nature of the bill itself. The anti-democratic attempt to force the law through the Scottish parliament in a matter of weeks was the final straw for a number of organisations who protested and forced the government to back down and reformulate the bill in a more considered manner. This confrontation faced by the government is all the more extraordinary when you consider that very few of these organisations actually opposed the principle of the bill itself.

Columnists like Iain MacWhirter of the Herald thought that Alex Salmond's grandstanding about the 'game of shame' was largely for show and would not result in an actual law being passed. Michael Fry of the Scotsman noted that some cases of attempted murder had led to prison sentences of five years, and to give the same length sentence to someone for being offensive at a football game could undermine the moral legitimacy of law. And yet here we are.

For many fans the law was seen as a joke, as relating to something that should never be seen as criminal let alone as an offence that should result in five years in prison. At games supporters made up songs mocking the SNP and exclaiming that 'supporting your team is not a crime'. Hundreds of comments on the petition set up to oppose the bill pointed with incredulity to comparable types of offences that could lead to prison sentences: Knife crimes, burglary, attempted rape, arson and so on. One comment noted that in theory you could offend someone at a game and the offended individual could find you afterwards and stab you, and you could end up with a longer prison sentence than the knife attacker.

The term 'grandstanding' is useful regarding the so called 'game of shame' and the subsequent political rhetoric and subsequent promotion of the

Offensive Behaviour Bill that followed on from it. From the off, the 'game of shame' was nothing out of the ordinary and had nothing to do with fans bad behaviour, and yet this game was used as the basis for setting up a football summit and demanding that something must be done about sectarianism. Despite the rhetorical focus on sectarianism, the new law, strangely, does not mention sectarianism once. If the problem was sectarianism, why is there no mention of it? Why have a new law when laws already exist to tackle it? One new dimension to the bill was that it would allow the police to target offensive songs sung by Celtic fans – to target what the chief police officers called 'political sectarianism'. There is an argument to be made for this and yet the argument was never made. Perhaps the government realised that there were directly problematic and anti-democratic issues associated with banning political songs. If so, this unwillingness to debate the issue is deceitful and cowardly.

Time and again sectarianism was held up as a major problem in Scotland, although little evidence was given for this claim. Where there was 'evidence', like the number of religiously aggravated offences, it was represented in a distorted and exaggerated way, more geared towards getting the right headline in the morning press than as part of an attempt to understand or tackle a serious social problem. As Graham Spiers insightfully observed in 1996, without the chance to express outrage about bigotry and our 'hate-filled city' the chattering classes in Scotland would feel 'stripped naked'. The same applies today except now the chatter is taking place in the Scottish Parliament and in senior police headquarters. As we noted earlier, the sectarian issue has become more important to the elite at precisely the time when any religious or political substance behind it has disappeared. For a fragile elite with few clear principles or powerful beliefs, fighting the straw man of sectarianism is a perfect way of masking the reality that the emperor has no clothes.

Despite the authoritarian nature of the Offensive Behaviour Act, with its five year maximum sentence, it is highly unlikely that anyone will ever get five years in prison under this law. Other observers have noted that you can actually give five year sentences using some of the existing laws and so even this part of the bill was adding nothing new. Again it appears that this length of sentence was another form of political grandstanding, a strange kind of performance, a way for Alex Salmond and the SNP to push out their chests and appear to be doing something serious and significant.

If we were to take Roseanna Cunningham and the SNP seriously and accept that this thing sectarianism was a serious problem in Scotland, would we really introduce a law that targeted only football fans? Why not start a political or a moral campaign to fight it rather than rely upon the police to enforce behaviour modification upon people? Shouting, 'It's wrong. Don't do it', and threatening people with prison is not the same as having a political or moral argument about a subject; it is in fact an abdication of both political and moral leadership.

But then, at one level, it is hard to believe the problem is being taken seriously if football is where we end up. Even with all the current elite prejudices about football fans, would anybody seriously believe that a social problem can be tackled during the 90 minutes of a game that only a small percentage of the population are involved in? Again the focus on football (in Scotland and indeed across the UK) appears to be both opportunistic and an avoidance of dealing with problems in the real world. It is easy to lecture to the working class when they are voluntarily trapped in camps known as a football ground. But this is a very strange place to try and make any serious political or moral points about anything – a place where fans shout and scream at men kicking a ball. This is after all a game we are talking about, not real life.

Perhaps this is why football attracts politicians – because the real world is a scary place and a much harder environment to manage. Football on the other hand is a regulators dream – the perfect place for an uninspiring behaviour manager to push his message. Standing watching the way fans behave, it is perhaps understandable why our regulators think there is a problem at games – but perhaps this is where they are at their most infantile – when they take football fans at their word. Supporters may be serious about football but that doesn't mean we should take football supporters seriously. The reason fans can be so passionate, so one sided and tribal, so aggressive, confrontational, crude, rude and at times obscene is because football is not real. Football fandom is pantomime for adults – to take what people say at games seriously reflects either a worrying naivety or a profound level of immaturity. To think you are challenging racism or sectarianism or indeed any 'ism' with your banners and stickers at football matches is a self aggrandising fantasy.

One final comment on the elites, and that is their incessant use of the word 'modern' as a catch-all term to indicate something that is good. We are told time and again that certain forms of behaviour are no longer acceptable in a 'modern' Scotland. The implication is that some things are from the past, are not modern, therefore they are backward, less civilised and less progressive than the new 'modern' way of behaving. But sticking the word modern in front of something doesn't make it progressive or forward looking. Indeed there are many important lessons and principles from history that are worth preserving – or indeed recreating. The classic ideas of freedom and liberty developed by John Stuart Mill in the nineteenth century are a case in point. The problem is that it takes strength of character and will to be genuinely tolerant, to accept the right of others to say things and behave in ways that offend you. Today the level of maturity needed in society to support genuine freedom and liberty is in short supply.

The alternative – Man Up!

At one level the alternative approach needed to develop a progressive political and cultural climate is very simple, and here it is. When you hear something you don't like or see someone behave in a way that offends you, have a word. If you're on the terraces and it's your opponents singing their song, sing your own songs louder. If it's one of your own fans being a racist or singing the (in my opinion) disgusting Hillsborough song, have a word. If there are tens of thousands of fans singing racist songs then things are a little different and you'll have to join or set up an anti-racist movement that seriously attempts to understand and tackle the root causes of racism. This is not as easy as running to the police, but it was and is the basis of how people have challenged ideas and attitudes they don't like for generations, and it is in the only genuine way to change things in society. Looking to the police to solve your 'offence' problems is a recipe for disaster.[89]

This is important not just for fans but also for players who are being educated to run to the authorities when they are offended. Whatever you think of John Terry and what he said, there is a problem that 'off the record' exchanges that go on during a match have become public property. As the football writer Duleep Allirajah argues, footballers will now have to be on their guard at all times, even during the heat of the battle when insults are often thrown at one another. In effect, he notes, 'footballers are [now] under perpetual police caution; what's said on the pitch may be used in evidence against them'.[90] Sadly the same can now be said about fans as well who must constantly look over their shoulder to check if what they are shouting has offended anybody. Despite some good intentions in all of this, the outcome is that the most basic aspect of solidarity and trust between players and fans is being destroyed.

In the Justice Committee discussion about the bill, fans representative Jeannette Findlay of the Celtic Supporters Trust explained that fans can be offensive but that doesn't mean they are criminal. Findlay is a robust character who strongly defended the right of Celtic fans to sing political songs and pointed out that it will simply be daft lads who have a drink and shout something or write something online who will end up being arrested and given a fine or a prison sentence and a criminal record that could destroy their hope of employment. Jeanette Findlay is right. Unfortunately, as someone on the left she believes that certain words and chants are not acceptable. The outcome of this position in law is that daft lads end up being criminalised, fining, imprisoned and given a criminal records for being drunk and shouting or writing something online that is seen as racist or sectarian. The vast majority of these individuals, it is worth reminding ourselves, as Graham Spiers noted, are 90 minute sectarians who couldn't be bigots if they tried – and yet these are the people that the bulk of the offence legislation effects.

It is not very long ago that even Rangers and Celtic die-hard supporters would not dream of reporting one another to the police. Today the trend is for both sides to do just that. 'Water off a duck's back' was an expectation that reflected a basic recognition by fans that what went on during a game was not to be taken seriously. Those who ended up in a fight deserved to be arrested because this was something completely different, a form of harm, as J.S. Mill would point out, which should not be accepted in a civilised society. The water off a duck's back sentiment also reflected a very basic expectation that adults should be able to deal with offensive language and behaviour and a belief that your opponents could and should do likewise. Being robust is a key part of developing self respect, it is likewise something that results in respect for others who illustrate a similar strength of character. Banter, and offenses thrown at games (or even in pubs) have historically been treated in this manner, where you are expected to take words 'on the chin', but this is changing and the offence legislation is in danger of creating a generation of men and women with glass jaws.

The exact type of behaviour that is and is not acceptable at games will change over time but this needs to be resolved by fans themselves. This means there will be people whose behaviour you find offensive, but this is part and parcel of being part of the public; it's called (or used to be called) real life.

Historically, Western societies and the enlightenment ideals developed in Scotland were predicated upon a recognition that for people to be free they also needed to be tough. Being a morally responsible individual, having to make your own way in an ever changing world is hard. Consequently, the 'free individual' was expected to be robust. Today this ideal has all but collapsed and society is increasingly institutionalising the vulnerable and chronically offended victim as the norm – indeed the good. Not surprisingly the basic freedoms previously expected in a democratic society are being lost.

On the petition against the new bill a number of fans made a case for free speech in football. Celtic fan Sean Conway argued that, 'This is a disgrace and it must stop now!! I hate Rangers on derby days but at times like this I will stand by them as fellow fans because together we can kick this bill out of our football!! HAIL HAIL'. At an Ibrox meeting I spoke at, a vote was taken to oppose the criminalisation of all songs, the 'motion' was passed by 85 to 5 votes. With many individuals and groups having an interest in the policing of and moralising about football fans the chances of changing today's authoritarian climate appears to be slight. However, as Mill has noted, individuals with genuine beliefs and convictions can take on an army of the petty minded who have only interests. For freedom and liberty to have any real meaning today we must demand that people in football and beyond 'Man Up'.

Afterword:
The New Sectarians

LOOKING AT THE SITUATION IN SCOTLAND, MUCH OF THIS BOOK HAS ATTEMPTED TO show that the problems being presented by the authorities are exaggerated and largely false. However, there are some new problems emerging and potentially much bigger problems to come. These problems are not related to any increase in old-fashioned bigotry or sectarianism, but are emerging because of a new kind of sectarian or sect-like behaviour being encouraged by the authorities themselves. This new 'sectarianism' relates to the rise of identity politics in Scotland and to the already growing importance of offensiveness and the protection of the offended; trends that are encouraging an insular, thin-skinned, tell-tale culture that could heighten divisions between fans.

For right-thinking people in football, *respect* is the buzz word. At the Euro 2012 tournament, it's hard to escape the advertising hoardings surrounding the ground and the 'Respect' logo on the shirt sleeves of every player. Within British football, respect is a shibboleth, but the idea of respect has a number of meanings. It can be about respecting referees and being sporting; it is also about tolerance and the respect of difference or diversity. The term incorporates basics concepts of etiquette, fair play and decent behaviour, often associated with the notion of footballers as role models, with seemingly more political ideas of anti-racism and anti-sectarianism. Respect has also become an institutionalised activity within football, involving children holding hands with players and players being made to shake hands before games, rather than, as they had done, shaking hands after the match. In terms of 'difference and diversity', the respect campaign captures well the transformation of anti-racism from a political issue to one of manners, of being respectful.[91] In all of these 'Respect' initiatives there is a certain school-marmish quality and a sense of performance, as footballers, for example, *act* as our role-models and are instructed about how to do thing 'in front of the children'.

The elevation of 'offence' within politics, culture and even law both reflects and creates a world where being offended becomes significant. As Joel Feinberg noted, we have moved from a society based on the harm principle to one based on the offence principle. In many respects, this appears to be a more caring approach – showing a concern about people's feelings and attempting to stop certain hurtful things being said. However, as we have seen with the criminalisation of football songs, a major consequence of this approach is that more things come to be seen as unacceptable and even against the law. The more society treats people as vulnerable and assumes we need to be protected from offence, the more it becomes authoritarian. As a result, society begins to resemble a school, with adults being treated like children who constantly need to be protected from one another and told how to behave. And, like children, we start to be genuinely outraged and 'hurt' by words that for previous generations would have been water off a duck's back.

In her excellent little book, *Talk to the Hand*, Lynne Truss describes a world where people live in their own bubble – *a hamster ball world*. Here, a modern day character type is formed – self preoccupied and totally disconnected from people around them. This character type has been educated to understand the world only with reference to his private emotions and consequently is profoundly inward looking and intensely asocial. This is an individual who experiences any form of questioning or challenge as a personal insult and threat to their 'self esteem'. The offence laws and initiatives actually help to protect and create this very type of person – antisocial narcissists who lacks any sense of camaraderie or solidarity with other people, engaged only by 'How I Feel', they are the hub of the chronically offended complainers, often found down at the local police station reporting their friends, neighbours and even family, for 'offences' against themselves.[92]

One glaring example of the antisocial nature of the 'dis-respected individual' came a few years ago in the form of David Appleman, a Jewish technology teacher who in 2007 reported his own students for racism after a YouTube clip showed them shouting the Spurs' 'Yid Army' chant. Following complaints to the police by Appleman, eight police officers turned up to Chauncy School and arrested a group of 15-16 year old boys on suspicion of racism. They were then fingerprinted, photographed and had DNA swabs taken, followed by nine hours of questioning. After releasing the youths on police bail, a Hertfordshire Police spokesman explained that, 'We take allegations of this nature very seriously and we believe we acted accordingly'.

What made this case all the more peculiar was that these boys were at the teacher's leaving party and he was filmed smiling and shaking hands with the boys while the chant was taking place. The term 'Yid army' itself may appear racist but is generally seen as a friendly chant used by Tottenham fans about the club's longstanding following amongst the Jewish community in north London. Whatever the ins and outs of the case, it is nevertheless a remarkable development for a member of a profession that encourages children to ignore name calling and to stand up to people who offend you, to act in this way. Here we have a teacher being 'offended' by his own pupils, to his face, and he goes and tells the police on them! If the boys were being insulting, which was probably not even their intention, Appleman could have challenged them himself or contacted senior teachers at the school if need be. Instead, he did the 'correct' thing and phoned the police. One has to ask, where is Mr Appleman's self respect? Indeed, where is his basic sense of adulthood?

David Appleman may be an extremely fragile individual, I don't know, but clearly society, the law and the police are now operating with this feeble, and indeed antisocial, model of adulthood as their norm. When a child tells tales on their friends, it is bad enough. But when an adult, a teacher, tells tales on his pupils – and to the police, who take it seriously – it is a worrying sign indeed. When society starts treating adults like children, grown men become infantilised and a tell-tale culture is the inevitable result.

If society educates us that 'words hurt', it is likely that they will do just that. When certain words are given priority treatment by the authorities and within the culture of society, they are likely to create a particularly acute response – the forging of offended people. Indeed, being thin skinned and being offended is the 'correct' response today, as the Evra-Suarez and the John Terry – Anton Ferdinand sagas illustrate. We expect and encourage people to be 'offended' and to report colleagues and fellow professionals to the authorities for name calling.

The new sectarians

In Scotland, being offended and reporting your fellow fan to the police has become institutionalised and is likely to become an increasing source of tension between fans – a new 'sectarian' divide. Kevin Rooney, in his article, 'Turning football fans into snitches', notes that despite the significant decline in 'offensive' songs at Old Firm matches, fans have taken to 'more sinister methods of playing out their hostility towards rival teams'. As he explains:

> Now we have the situation where fans are using new media including YouTube, Twitter and Facebook to monitor the behaviour of rivals and expose every expression of sectarianism or 'offensive' remarks made.[93]

Old football rivalries inevitably led to significant tensions between fans; they hated one another, even fought one another. But despite this rivalry, never before would it have been seen as acceptable to call in the police to get opposing fans arrested and imprisoned because you don't like what they say at games. As Stirling University student, Lee Dunlop found out to his cost, this norm is no longer the case. Dunlop was reported to the police by fellow students for posting a comic picture of himself on Facebook. For his end of term party, Lee Dunlop dressed up as Postman Pat carrying a bomb addressed to Neil Lennon. This 'offensive image' resulted in Dunlop being arrested and held in a cell overnight. Thankfully, on this occasion, the religiously-aggravated charge was dropped and Dunlop was able to remain at his university. In future, others may not be so lucky.

Before the Offensive Behaviour Act dragged Celtic fans into the orbit of 'offence', it was largely Rangers fans that were targeted for their particular form of offensiveness. In 2011, the chief of security at Ibrox even complained about the excessive scrutiny Rangers were receiving from the Policing Football Unit, arguing that, 'The unit has attended 100 percent of our matches this season, often filming fans, including children, who are not engaging in any offensive behaviours. We are unaware of any other club that the unit has so far attended 100 percent of their matches' (*Daily Record* 31st August 2011).

Rangers Football Club and fans have come under severe pressure in the last decade from a plethora of sources to stop singing certain songs. The criminalisation of religious and racially based terms has meant that Rangers fans have noticeably changed the songs they sing. The variant of the 'Billy Boys' song incorporating the line about being up to your knees in 'Fenian blood' is noticeably absent from games today, as are other songs and chants that can be labelled as racist or sectarian.

A major source of anger amongst some Rangers fans about the criminalisation of their songs is that they believe Celtic Football Club and their fans, have acted as 'grasses' for the last ten years, reporting Rangers fans to the authorities and trying to get songs outlawed. After a press release I sent out in 2011 arguing that the Old Firm should unite to defeat the Offensive Behaviour Bill, the response from some Rangers fans was one of outrage and incredulity. A debate erupted on one particular Rangers fan site about this call for unity. Below are a few of the responses made about the press release:

- Sorry but reap what you sow, their mob brought this s**t on with complaints and the media complaining about the big bad huns (sectarian in its own right) but when the spotlight shines on their song sheet then you're being 'persecuted'??? Sorry but if it wasn't for the mortally offended Celtic support this knee jerk reaction by the government wouldn't be in the pipelines. I don't agree with the legislation but remember who brought this on, Celtic FC and their forever offended fans. We're already being persecuted for our song book, we have been under the spotlight for over 10 years (BarLoch76).
- Most Rangers fans were perfectly happy to let Celtic fans sing what they wanted (which doesn't mean we like it) provided we could do the same. The Celtic-minded would not play the game though. Our rivals are twisted and untrustworthy (GioVabB).
- In short they caused this problem, but now they are being watched, they need us to dig them out of the hole they created (Mexi).
- If this legislation got thrown in the bin in its entirety where would this leave us? With the status quo where Rangers fans alone are exposed to every single complaint made from an orchestrated campaign. We've been singing solo for years now (Hyramotyre).
- The rest of Scotland sat back and let Rangers supporters be vilified and prosecuted (Hillheadbear).

For some Rangers fans, the Celtic supporters cannot be trusted to fight for fans' freedoms as they are seen as the ones who have pushed for laws and regulations of songs at games; as BarLoch76 argues, they brought this 's**t on'. Looking at the history of the legislation introduced in Scotland to regulate fans, these Rangers supporters have a point. Various high-profile Celtic supporters and members of Celtic Football Club have argued for, and supported, legislation to outlaw some of Rangers' songs. Some fans have also helped to encourage new legislation by complaining about Rangers fans to the authorities.

The example of the 'Famine Song' is a case in point because it was a Celtic fan who first complained to the Irish Consul about this song. Following this, Celtic chairman and former home secretary John Reid argued that the song was in breach of race-relations legislation. Joe Bradley from Celtic Minded argued that the continued singing of the 'Famine Song' showed Scotland had not moved on from sectarianism. Meanwhile, MP and Celtic supporter George Galloway demanded that the police should act to stop this 'hate anthem' being sung.

Ironically, it appears that the 'Famine Song' was invented by Rangers fans as a direct response to the anti-sectarian industry established at the start of this century, and specifically in relation to the religiously aggravated charge introduced in the 2003 Criminal Justice (Scotland) Act. The song itself is purposefully offensive, but manages to avoid any religious and therefore potentially sectarian words. Nevertheless, it was defined in law as 'racist' and consequently became another song Rangers fans could not sing – further intensifying the anger amongst some fans who once again saw Celtic and Celtic fans as 'grasses', responsible for getting Rangers fans arrested for simply singing offensive songs.

Despite some Celtic supporters having encouraged the criminalisation of Rangers songs, it is nevertheless a mistake to understand this development as something that has been created by 'their' side. The anti-sectarian and the 'offence' industry both go to the heart of the new elites and their approach to regulating public life. The bizarre example of the 'Famine Song' being labelled racist and criminal is not particularly illustrative of the persuasive powers of Celtic supporters. It reflects, rather, the changing and increasingly flexible framework of 'offensiveness' and the growing use of law to regulate and enforce 'correct' behaviour in society in general and for football fans in particular.

Nevertheless, the culture of complaint where fans take on the persona of the offended victim is an important and a worrying indication of a breakdown in basic solidarity between even rival fans.

You're offended? I'm offended!

Talking to Celtic fans, they are clear that at least some of the more Loyalist Rangers fans in the past would have happily supported a ban on IRA songs. Today, many Rangers fans take a relatively principled position on the freedom of fans to sing their songs. This is in part because they themselves have experienced the consequences of having their songs and chants regulated and banned. However, when Celtic FC and their fans became the target of the authorities, some Rangers fans reacted in a sectarian fashion and celebrated. After the Rennes game when Celtic were reported to UEFA by the police for 'illicit' chanting, a number of Rangers fans websites contained comments of support for this development:

What's good for one etc etc.

About time.

Great decision!

What goes around and what not.

This reaction was partly in response to the unfairness felt by Rangers fans to their songs being targeted while Celtic's IRA type songs were not. This decision would at least, in their mind, 'balance things up'. However, as Kevin Rooney observed, it is not only Celtic fans who have acted as 'snitches', with for example, 'hundreds of Rangers fans' reporting Neil Lennon to the police 'for making supposedly racist remarks to Rangers' controversial player El-Hadji Diouf'. Following this 'snitching' by Rangers fans, lip readers were brought in to study TV footage and Lennon was questioned by the police.[94]

The online Celtic site ETims has also correctly observed that there has been rank hypocrisy from sections of the media. Jim Traynor of the *Daily Record*, for example, has argued that banning Rangers football chants, 'will threaten our right to free speech', but appears keen to have the 'miserable, moronic minority' of Celtic fans censored by the offence police.[95]

With the passing of the Offensive Behaviour Act, the framework for the new sectarianism is firmly established and all fans will now be encouraged to find offence in their opponent's songs and behaviour. Mark Dingwall of the Rangers Supporters Trust made this very point at the Justice Committee discussion on the bill in the Scottish Parliament when he observed that everything was now up for grabs in terms of being offended. Dingwall oscillates between wanting other fans to be treated as harshly as Rangers have been, especially Celtic fans, and recognising that there is an 'air of unreality' about the creation of a chronically offended climate. As he observed, 'Now we have a situation where there's almost an incitement to escalate your offendedness'.[96] Speaking at the *Battle of Ideas* in London, Mark Dingwall explained that:

It's turned us, me, into a grass...What we're doing is handcuffing ourselves to Aberdeen fans and Celtic fans and saying if you find things we say offensive we are going to start complaining about you. People are literally sitting there with stop-watches and videoing games...you write to the match commander, you write to the police because that's the only way we see we can get out of this corner is to handcuff ourselves to other fans and pull them over the edge with us.[97]

This new sectarianism is sanctioned by the state and is one of the most worrying developments in Scottish football and perhaps even in Scottish society more widely. We now have a situation where the most anti-social and self-preoccupied, chronically offended individual has become the model citizen. The likely outcome is that complaints to the police about an increasing array of 'offensive' comments will rise. This reporting is likely to be about not only opposition fans but also fans of your own team. Indeed, some fans are already doing just that. Some Celtic fans, for example, are no longer arguing the toss about the rights and wrongs of singing Irish Republican songs at games and instead make complaints to stewards and the police about other Celtic fans singing IRA songs.[98] Indeed, clubs across the UK are starting to hand out leaflets advising their very own hamster ball fans to 'call this number' and report the seat number of the fan you find offensive.

As the offence bandwagon becomes a runaway train, the 'snitching' on fellow fans, and the squealing antics of 'dis-respected' fellow professional footballers, spirals ever further out of control.

At the same time, in Scotland, there is also the likelihood that the minority of old-fashioned sectarians will now spend their time searching the internet to find offensive words written by people they hate. As one editorial comment noted, the new law can actually give the moral right to bigots to express their intolerance by being offended (*Scotland on Sunday* 26th June 2011). Law is often a blunt instrument to deal with social problems; when it is backed by an unthinking 'zero tolerance' approach, the potential for unintended and reactionary outcomes is escalated further.

One final outcome of the Offensive Behaviour Act worth mentioning is that pub landlords are now being squeezed to prevent and even report offensive songs or chants in their pubs. Not surprisingly, there has been a reaction to this from pub owners who will no longer be able to use their judgement about how people are behaving in their establishment; now they will be forced to act like police. Consequently, codes of behaviour established in different pubs over generations are suddenly lost as informal mechanisms for mucking along with other people disappear and everyday life is colonised by official codes of conduct. In essence, what is happening in these 'public houses', as they were once known, has and is happening in football grounds: the self regulation of fans is being wiped out, to be replaced by intense surveillance and state censoring.

Victim Identity

As we discussed earlier, 'offensiveness' was clearly important to the new football legislation introduced in 2012, and was something that codified a wider trend in society – the protection of the public from being offended. In many respects, the Offensive Behaviour Act codified a pecking order of outrage, specifying particular groups who needed to be protected from offence. The Scottish Council of Jewish Communities argued that there was a danger that the bill would create a 'hierarchy of discrimination' (*Scotsman* 25th June 2011). Women, for example, are not one of the 'protected' groups in the act, something that has been questioned with respect to this law and, indeed, in relation to hate crime more generally. Why are gay people a specially-protected group, but not women? In the USA, the development of hate crime laws saw an ever-increasing competition amongst interest groups for special 'offence' status. The same process is emerging in Scotland.

Part of the process of criminalising 'hate' involves the categorising of particularly offended or vulnerable groups who need special protection. One outcome of this is that campaigners and paid representatives of certain defined 'groups' or 'cultures' systematically attempt to prove that they are being offended. Again, a newer form of sect-like behaviour subsequently evolves as these special interest groups clamour to demonstrate the lack of respect being shown to their culture. Indeed, this was evident in the discussion stages of the Offensive Behaviour Bill and in the written submissions to the Justice Committee. Even organisations representing children felt the need to explain the victimised nature of their 'group' who were particularly affected by 'sectarian bullying'.

Within the Old Firm, it is Celtic fans that are categorised by their opponents as being victims – as mortally or 'forever offended' – making claims about the unfair treatment of not only Celtic Football Club but Catholics or the 'Scots Irish'. Today, however, Rangers fans are also likely to adopt a victim identity and to represent opposing sentiments as offensive to their 'culture' or 'tradition'.

On the Strathclyde Police Facebook site concerns about Celtic songs have been raised by Rangers fans in an attempt to get them banned. John McDougall Senior, for instance, asked if the police would stop Celtic fans singing 'Roll of Honour' because, 'it must be very upsetting for anyone who has lost a loved one'. Members of Rangers Supporters Trust made similar arguments to me about the upsetting nature of some Celtic songs for those in the crowd who had relatives killed in Northern Ireland. In a Trust statement about the '*Famine Song*', it is the 'abuse' of members of the Royal Family that is discussed. Therapeutic and victim-centred language is used to explain how Celtic's offensive songs are upsetting, perhaps even traumatising. Indeed, Rangers fans' celebration of the British Army is increasingly couched in non-political, even non-nationalistic terms today (a trend seen more widely in Britain as a whole) with 'our boys' themselves being represented as hard done to victims rather than proud fighters and defenders of Britain and British interests abroad.

The multicultural Old Firm?

Part of the shift towards a victim identity has come with the transformation of religious and political beliefs and loyalties associated with clubs like Rangers and Celtic into 'traditions' and 'cultures'. Almost any outlook or 'tradition' across the UK can now be defended through the argument that 'it's my culture'. For example, the singer Billy Bragg has suggested that left-wing people should stop challenging the anti-democratic nature of the Royal Family, and respect monarchists as another aspect of multiculturalism. On a Radio Four debate, discussing the Queen's Diamond Jubilee, a Unionist politician from Northern Ireland put a Sinn Fein spokesperson on the defensive by demanding that he should respect his Queen – after all, it is 'my culture'. Even the British National Party defend their views today by using the language of multiculturalism.

The shift towards understanding people as part of a 'culture', rather than as individuals with ideas and beliefs, has escalated in the last two decades and could potentially develop much further in Scotland – creating a new divide between the 'British Rangers' *tradition* and the 'Irish Celtic' *culture*. Discussing

the 'Scots Irish', academic John Kelly describes the Catholic/Celtic part of
Scotland as an 'ethnic' group, and uses analogies to equate the treatment
of black people with that of the ethnic Scots Irish. Despite accepting that
structurally – in terms of jobs, services, housing and so on – there is little or
no discrimination against Catholics in Scotland, Kelly talks about 'attitudinal'
sectarianism. Denying the ethnic identity of the 'Scots Irish' consequently
becomes understood as a form of racism. Once the 'Scots Irish' are established
as a 'culture' in this way, the trend is to demand recognition for your identity
and also to search for examples where this respect is not forthcoming. As a
result, academics like John Kelly are keen to discover and promote examples of
the mistreatment of the Scots Irish, incorrectly using the figures on religiously-
aggravated offences, for example, to 'prove' that Catholics in Scotland are being
abused and even oppressed. Protecting the cultural identity of the Scots Irish
is turned into a mission by Kelly's approach, and those who disrespect this
identity will need to be silenced.[99]

In his fascinating *From Fatwa to Jihad*, Kenan Malik traces the development
of multicultural policies in England. He notes, in particular, how the political
identity of being 'black' in the 1980s was transformed, in part, through state-
sponsored initiatives that engaged with and encouraged the emergence of
separate cultural identities. Rather than having self defined 'black' people
fighting against racism, the state sponsored 'respectable' and conservative
sections of the newly-framed 'Muslim', or 'Afro-Caribbean' *communities* to set up
their own organisations, community centres, initiatives and so on. One of the
results of this was that even black people in Britain became compartmentalised
into narrowly-defined static *identities* around which political and financial
claims could be made to the state. Once political power and financial resources
became allocated by ethnicity, Malik explains, 'people began to identify
themselves in terms of their ethnicity, and *only* their ethnicity'. Conflict now
emerged not in terms of political struggles for equality, but in relation to the
demand that 'my culture' is respected. Malik notes how 'difference' became
felt more acutely than commonality and a defence of one's tradition resulted
in the search for examples of disrespect being shown. This resulted in a newly
politicised form of 'hurt' being experienced and demands made by groups that
the state step in to prevent offence being shown to different cultures. These
developments were significantly influenced by left-wing Labour councils
who shifted away from a fight for social equality to one of defending cultural
difference. As he argues, 'Multiculturalism helped create new divisions and
more intractable conflicts which made for a less openly racist but a more
insidiously tribal Britain'.[100] One result of this was that offence claims
increased and explosive expressions of 'hurt' erupted; for example, the claim
was made that Salman Rushdie's *The Satanic Verses* meant the 'annihilation' of
the Muslim cultural identity, with Rushdie's book being publically burned by
members of the newly constructed, and offended, 'Muslim community'.

An important question to consider is whether the development and promotion of different 'cultures' in Scotland could encourage a similar or at least more significant divide emerging here. The recent development of multiculturalism in Northern Ireland is worth noting in this respect. In the past, the British authorities would argue that there could be equality for all British citizens, including Catholics, in Northern Ireland. Irish Republicans disagreed, pointed to the endemic inequality that existed in the North, and countered British claims by arguing that a united Ireland was essential for the freedom and equality for *all*, including Protestants. Today, in comparison, even the belief or aim of equality has been lost and the Northern Ireland Assembly itself embodies the need to provide specific recognition (or 'respect') for the different, separate, 'communities'. For example, no one group can hold the positions of both First Minister and Deputy First Minister and these positions must be shared between Unionist and Nationalist parties. In essence, the assembly assumes that there are two intractable communities who are and forever will need separate representation. Past political claims of universalism – or a potential common humanity (from both sides) are thus replaced by the invention of these static, ever-lasting unionist and nationalist 'communities' who must now learn to respect one another's difference. As Kevin Rooney notes, 'Far from overcoming and dissolving differences, the peace process had encouraged us to champion them and preserve then into the future'.[101]

Previously, I argued that claims about Scotland being just like Northern Ireland in terms of sectarianism were nonsense. However, it is possible that the new sectarianism in Scotland could emerge around different 'traditions' and 'cultures'.

Speculatively, it is possible to imagine a situation in Scotland where the 'celebration of difference' and the inclination to adopt cultural identities will encourage a new form of divide between some Irish-Celtic and British-Rangers fans. This is especially possible when the state encourages 'group identities' and gives support and protection to those who can act as a particular 'community'. The fact that the '*Famine Song*' has already been defined as 'racist' in Scotland illustrates the acceptance and promotion of the idea of there being different peoples – different 'races' even – amongst the white population of Scotland.

As an aside, one final irony of the '*Famine Song*' when looking at the issue of racism is that, in the past, people who campaigned against racism would often join anti-deportation campaigns to oppose black people being sent 'home' through the use of Britain's racist immigration laws that targeted certain groups and labelled them as 'illegal immigrants'. Today people (generally black people) continue to be sent 'home' but there are few if any campaigns against this anymore. At the same time, in Scotland, simply singing that people should 'go home' results in the charge of racism and subsequent police and state action against you.

Of course, for most Scots, life goes on, and 'cultural difference' has little or no meaning to a largely white, Scottish, secular society: Scotland is not Northern Ireland and multiculturalism will not develop here in such an obtuse separatist form. Nevertheless, the self-indulgent narcissist and the equally chronically offended sensibility of identity-conscious individuals intermingle and provide a basis for escalating offence claims in society. This becomes all the more likely when 'tolerance' is such an important governing framework within politics and when law is underwriting the encouragement of offence claims.

Constructing 'victim groups', or encouraging individuals and organisations to promote their 'cause' with reference to their victim status, has both divisive and authoritarian consequences. For example, gay and transgender individuals are given protected status in the new Offensive Behaviour Act. However, illustrating the way new legislation can open ever more doors with which to claim 'offence', gay rights groups raised questions about why only football fans were being targeted. Following the logic of the 'Offensive' Act, Tim Hopkins of the LGBT network asked why football fans being offensive online would be prosecuted while other homophobic comments, websites and Facebook pages called, for example, 'Kill the Gays', would not (*Scotsman* 25th June 2011). Hopkins is right – at least at the level of logic and fairness. Why criminalise only offensive football fans? If we are going to accept the importance and seriousness of offensiveness, surely anyone being offensive online should be arrested? If the logic of this argument is accepted, other individuals and groups will necessarily demand that the same rule apply to them, and so the continual spiral of offence winds ever further away from a society where free speech has any meaning.

Today people are being educated to be offended. Within football, as we have seen, one result of these developments is that counter claims amongst football fans emerge; they 'handcuff' themselves to opposing fans, and attempt to 'pull them over the edge'. This development at Old Firm games in particular is all the more unnecessary and ridiculous given the lack of depth to the 'sectarianism' that exists today. In the past, it could be argued that 'sectarian' chants at Old Firm games had weight and significance because there was a religious, and more importantly, a political situation or background giving wider meaning to them. Today this is no longer the case, and ironically it is the anti-sectarian industry, the construction of 'cultures' and the elevation of 'offence' that gives weight to words. Power is *given* to the words by the victim framework within which they are now interpreted – to words that today carry no social or political significance. These are zombie terms reanimated by the 'offence' legislation and promoted by an aggressive form of victimhood.

Finally, it is worth noting that despite their differences – the tolerance laws in Scotland, the outrage at 'intolerance' and the authorities' attempt to stamp down on offensiveness – can be seen as a mirror image of the outrage shown by Muslims in the 1980s towards Salman Rushdie's book *The Satanic Verses*. These protesting Muslims were also offended by words they did not like, this offensiveness could not be tolerated – indeed, they literally took a zero-tolerance approach and set the book on fire. Similarly, for the Scottish government, certain songs, chants and online comments are offensive, they cannot be tolerated and a zero tolerance attitude means they must be banned. More recently, it is images that have offended some Muslims and led to protests and more burnings, this time of a Muhammad cartoon in a Danish newspaper. In Scotland, we too have seen the image of Lee Dunlop dressed as Postman Pat causing outrage and offense, leading to an arrest and the effective outlawing of this image. Like the 'extremist' Muslims who will not tolerate images or words they find offensive, in 2011, Roseanna Cunningham, Alex Salmond and the rest of the Scottish National Party established themselves as our champions of intolerance – they became the equivalent of Scotland's very own book burners.

Bibliography

Ashworth, A. (1995) 'Criminalising Disrespect', in *Criminal Law Review*. Vol. 98.

Bailin, A. (2011) 'Criminalising free speech?' in *Criminal Law Review*. Vol. 9, pp705-711.

Brick, C. (1999) 'Upfront', *Offence*, Issue 4, Spring/Summer.

Brick, C. (2000) 'Taking Offence', in *Soccer and Society*. Vol. 1, Issue. 1.

Bruce, S., Glendinning, T., Paterson, I. and Rosie, M. (2004) *Sectarianism in Scotland*. Edinburgh: Edinburgh University Press.

Collins, M. (2004) *The Likes of Us: A Biography of the White Working Class*. London: Granta Books.

Flint, J. (2008) Governing Sectarianism in Scotland. *Scottish Affairs*. No. 63, spring, pp. 120-137.

Furedi, F. (2011) *On Tolerance: A Defence of Moral Independence*. London: Continuum

Garland, J. and Rowe, Michael. (1999) 'Policing Racism at Football Matches', in *International Journal of the Sociology of Law*. Vol. 27.

Giulianotti, R., Bonney, N. & Hepworth, M. (1994) *Football Violence and Social Identity*. London: Routledge.

Goodall, K. (2011) *Edinburgh Law Review*. Vol. 15, pp.423-427.

Greenfield, S. and Osborn, G. (2001) *Regulating Football: Commodification, Consumption and the Law*. London: Pluto.

Hall, E. B. (2009) *The Friends of Voltaire*. South Carolina: BiblioBazaar.

Jacobs, J. and Potter, K. (1998) *Hate Crime: Criminal Law and Identity Politics*. Oxford: Oxford University Press.

Jacoby, R. (1999) *The End of Utopia: Politics and Culture in an Age of Apathy*. New York: Basic Books.

Kyriakides, C. & Torres, R. (2012) 'The Allure of race: From New Lefts to New Times', in *New Political Science*. Vol. 31:1, pp. 55-80.

Kyriakides, C. (2008) 'Third Way Anti-Racism', in *Ethnic and Racial Studies*. Vol. 31, No. 3, pp.592-610.

Loewenberg, S. (2006) 'Fears of World Cup sex trafficking boom unfounded', in *The Lancet*. Vol. 368, Issue 9530.

Malik, K. (2009) *From Fatwa to Jihad: The Rushdie Affair and its Legacy*. London: Atlantic Books.

Marx, K. (1970) *The German Ideology*. London: Lawrence and Wishart.

McArdle, D. (2000) *From Boot Money to Bosman: Football Society and the Law*. London: Cavendish.

Mill, J. S. (1975) *Three Essays: On Liberty; Representative Government; The Subjection of Women*. Oxford: Oxford University.

Rosie, M. (2004) *The Sectarian Myth in Scotland: Of bitter memory and bigotry*. Hampshire: Palgrave Macmillan.

Truss, L. (2005) *Talk to the Hand: The Utter Bloody Rudeness of Everyday Life*. New York: Gotham.

Voltaire (1924) *The Philosophical Dictionary* translated by H. I. Woolf. New York: Knopf.

Žižek, S. (2009) *Violence*. London: Profile.

Endnotes

1] See http://www.scotland.gov.uk/News/Releases/2011/06/17085318

2] See http://www.scotland.gov.uk/News/Releases/2011/11/18120149

3] McArdle, D. (2000) *From Boot Money to Bosman: Football Society and the Law*. London: Cavendish. pp. 67.

4] McArdle (2000: 67).

5] Giulianotti, R., Bonney, N. & Hepworth, M. (1994) *Football Violence and Social Identity*. London: Routledge. Chapter 1.

6] Greenfield, S. and Osborn, G. (2001) *Regulating Football: Commodification, Consumption and the Law*. London: Pluto. pp. 1.

7] See http://www.spiked-online.com/index.php/site/article/11179/

8] Andrew Ashworth (1995) 'Criminalising Disrespect', in *Criminal Law Review*, 98.

9] Brick, C. (1999) 'Upfront', *Offence*, Issue 4, Spring/Summer.

10] Garland, J. and Rowe, M. (1999) 'Policing Racism at Football Matches', in *International Journal of the Sociology of Law*. 27, pp. 225.

11] McArdle, D. (2000: 82).

12] Giulianotti, R., Bonney, N. & Hepworth, M. (1994: 24).

13] Brick, C. (2000) 'Taking Offence', in *Soccer and Society*, Vol. 1, Issue. 1.

14] Brick, C. (2000: 161).

15] As above.

16] See chapter 4 of *From Boot Money to Bosman*.

17] See for example, Kyriakides, C. & Torres, R. (2012) 'The Allure of race: From New Lefts to New Times', in *New Political Science*. 31:1, pp. 55-80.

18] See McArdle (2000: Appendix 1).

19] See http://www.spiked-online.com/index.php/site/article/10861/

20] See www.spiked-online.com/index.php/site/article/1836

21] Garland and Rowe (1999: 225).

22] See www.spiked-online.com/index.php/site/article/10861

23] See www.spiked-online.com/index.php/site/article/11947

24] Kyriakides, C. (2008) 'Third Way Anti-Racism', in *Ethnic and Racial Studies*. Vol. 31, No. 3, pp.592-610.

25] See www.spiked-online.com/index.php/site/article/10861

26] See http://www.spiked-online.com/index.php/site/printable/12064/

27] See BBC website http://www.bbc.co.uk/news/uk-scotland-glasgow-west-15155641

28] See BBC website http://www.bbc.co.uk/news/uk-scotland-glasgow-west-15333744

29] See *Spectator* CoffeeHouse 18th October 2011 or online http://www.spectator.co.uk/alexmassie/7320834/stephen-birrells-conviction-shames-scotland.thtml

30] See the Equalities and Human Rights Commission submission to the Scottish Parliament's Justice Committee.

31] See the Scottish Government website http://www.scotland.gov.uk/
Publications/2011/07/22120711/1

32] See BBC online http://www.bbc.co.uk/news/uk-scotland-glasgow-west-
14632440

33] See Flint, J. (2008) Governing Sectarianism in Scotland. *Scottish Affairs*, no. 63,
spring, pp. 120-137.

34] Flint (2008: 130).

35] See the Scottish Government website http://www.scotland.gov.uk/Topics/
Justice/crimes/8978

36] See the online *Hate Crime Guidance Manual* 2010.

37] Jacobs, J. and Potter, K. (1998) *Hate Crime: Criminal Law and Identity Politics*.
Oxford: Oxford University Press

38] Kay Goodall (2011) *Edinburgh Law Review*. Vol. 15, pp. 423-427.

39] In reality Mr Harris does not actually support free speech at football but was
happy to be associated with opposition to the new bill.

40] See the online SPICe Briefing: Offensive Behaviour at Football and
Threatening Communications (Scotland) Bill: Stage 3, p. 16.

41] Brick (2000) 'Taking Offence', in *Soccer and Society*, Vol. 1, Issue. 1. pp.168.

42] Brick (2000: 169).

43] See http://news.bbc.co.uk/1/hi/scotland/glasgow_and_west/7617518.stm

44] See http://news.bbc.co.uk/sport1/hi/football/europe/4907724.stm

45] Bailin, A. (2011) 'Criminalising free speech?' in *Criminal Law Review*, vol. 9,
pp705-711.

46] Bailin (2011: 710)

47] See http://standpointmag.co.uk/node/4257/full

48] See http://www.spiked-online.com/index.php/site/article/12271/"http://
www.spiked-online.com/index.php/site/article/12271/

49] See for example http://www.heraldsun.com.au/news/more-news/uk-
looters-and-rioters-face-court/story-e6frf7lf-1226113427402

50] See http://www.spiked-online.com/index.php/site/printable/11909/

51] See http://www.spiked-online.com/index.php/site/article/10979/"http://
www.spiked-online.com/index.php/site/article/10979/

52] See for example *The Likes of Us: A Biography of the White Working Class* by Michael
Collins, Grant Books (2004).

53] See http://stumblingandmumbling.typepad.com/stumbling_and_
mumbling/2007/01/cbb_shooting_th.html"http://stumblingandmumbling.
typepad.com/stumbling_and_mumbling/2007/01/cbb_shooting_th.html

54] See www.spiked-online.com/index.php?/site/article/424

55] Loewenberg, S. (2006) 'Fears of World Cup sex trafficking boom unfounded',
in *The Lancet*, Vol. 368, Issue 9530, pp.105-6.

56] See www.spiked-online.com/index.php?/site/article/2850

57] http://www.scotland.gov.uk/News/Releases/2011/03/08163336

58] Of course, in a society that has shifted from the harm principle to the offence principle and one that polices the public accordingly, the very meaning of domestic violence has changed. As Lord Advocate Frank Mulholland spelled out when he explained that, 'We would like to reassure the public that we take crimes of domestic abuse, whether it is physical or emotional, extremely seriously'. Like the policing of offensive words at games, here we see the expanding therapeutic and authoritarian role of the police and state into the emotional lives people in Scotland. See,http://www.copfs.gov.uk/News/Releases/2011/09/Football-No-Excuse-Domestic-Abuse-says-Law-Enforcement

59] See http://news.stv.tv/scotland/west-central/232549-old-firm-crime-statistics/

60] The quote is from the footnotes from On Liberty. For an online source see http://www.econlib.org/library/Mill/mlLbtyNotes.html" http://www.econlib.org/library/Mill/mlLbtyNotes.html

61] See http://www.holyrood.com/articles/2011/11/18/strathclyde-is-bigotry-hotspot-as-religious-hate-rimes-increase/"http://www.holyrood.com/articles/2011/11/18/strathclyde-is-bigotry-hotspot-as-religious-hate-rimes-increase/

62] Bruce, S., Glendinning, T., Paterson, I. and Rosie, M. (2004) *Sectarianism in Scotland*. Edinburgh: Edinburgh University Press.

63] See http://www.glasgow.gov.uk/NR/rdonlyres/DA614F81-4F1B-4452-8847-F3FDE920D550/0/sectarianismo3.pdf"http://www.glasgow.gov.uk/NR/rdonlyres/DA614F81-4F1B-4452-8847-F3FDE920D550/0/sectarianismo3.pdf

64] Bruce et al (2004: 153).

65] Discussing the recent Royal Wedding a *Scotsman* columnist summed up the new approach of the cultural elite noting snidely that, 'I'd be lying if I claimed to regard it as anything more that a day off work and an opportunity to make sarcastic comments at the television' (*Scotsman* 30th December 2011).

66] See Chapter 4 'Ulster, Football and Violence' in Bruce, S., Glendinning, T., Paterson, I. and Rosie, M. (2004) *Sectarianism in Scotland*. Edinburgh: Edinburgh University Press.

67] Bruce et al (2004: 142).

68] Bruce et al (2004: 143)

69] See Kuper, S. (1994) *Football Against the Enemy*. London: Orion 1994, pp.205.

70] See http://news.bbc.co.uk/1/hi/northern_ireland/424217.stm"http://news.bbc.co.uk/1/hi/northern_ireland/424217.stm

71] See http://www.scotland.gov.uk/Topics/Justice/law/sectarianism-action-1/Education

72] This Lexis Nexis newspaper search starts in 1992 with the *Herald* and 1993 the *Scotsman* and *Scotland on Sunday*. The search was for any article containing both the terms 'Old Firm' and 'sectarian'.

73] See the video debate at http://news.bbc.co.uk/democracylive/hi/scotland/newsid_9582000/9582406.stm

74] Rosie, M. (2004) *The Sectarian Myth in Scotland: Of bitter memory and bigotry*. Hampshire: Palgrave Macmillan. pp. 144.

75] In 2010 Cara Henderson was still being interviewed about Mark Scott's death, the STV programme entitles, 'Cara Henderson – Lost her friend to Old Firm', introduced the issue by stating that, like Romeo and Juliette, 'one parallel with modern Scotland and 16th century Verona, West of Scotland sectarianism was every bit as blind and primitive as the feud between Shakespeare's Copulates and Montagues'. The role of *Nil by Mouth* clearly is to educate all of the 'primitive' sectarians who are represented by the murder of Mark Scott.

76] See http://www.scotland.gov.uk/Publications/2005/04/2193449/34509"http://www.scotland.gov.uk/Publications/2005/04/2193449/34509

77] See http://www.scotland.gov.uk/Resource/Doc/160254/0043618.pdf"http://www.scotland.gov.uk/Resource/Doc/160254/0043618.pdf

78] Flint, J. (2008) Governing Sectarianism in Scotland. *Scottish Affairs*, no. 63, spring, pp. 120-137.

79] See http://www.scotland.gov.uk/Publications/2006/12/11144623/2

80] The Orwell quote is in chapter 5 of the Furedi book, many of the other points raised here are discussed in Furedi, F. (2011) On Tolerance. London: Continuum.

81] Furedi, F. (2011) *On Tolerance: A Defence of Moral Independence*. London: Continuum

82] See http://www.scotland.gov.uk/Publications/2005/11/2192152/21544

83] Furedi (2011: 10).

84] Jacoby, R. (1999) *The End of Utopia: Politics and Culture in an Age of Apathy*. New York: Basic Books. pp. 31.

85] Jacoby (1999: 32-33).

86] See http://www.spiked-online.com/index.php/site/reviewofbooks_printable/12384/

87] See http://www.spiked-online.com/site/article/12552/"http://www.spiked-online.com/site/article/12552/

88] See http://www.thefreesociety.org/Columnists/Stuart-Waiton/the-moral-maze-of-free-speech"http://www.thefreesociety.org/Columnists/Stuart-Waiton/the-moral-maze-of-free-speech

89] At the same time of course it is worth noting that much, indeed most of what is said at football games is not to be taken seriously.

90] See http://www.spiked-online.com/site/article/12504/

91] The 2010 World Cup in South Africa captures the nature of official anti-racism perfectly. Here we had captains of teams that had reached the quarter finals forced to read out unthinkingly a Stalinist-like script about the badness of racism to the hundreds of millions of viewing fans. Anti-racism here becomes a formulaic mantra, no longer an issue discussed or challenged by our political leaders but literally chanted by our new 'role models'.

92] Truss, L. (2005) *Talk to the Hand*: The Utter Bloody Rudeness of Everyday Life. New York: Gotham.

93] See http://www.spiked-online.com/index.php/site/article/10448/"http://www.spiked-online.com/index.php/site/article/10448/

94] See http://www.spiked-online.com/index.php/site/article/10448/"http://www.spiked-online.com/index.php/site/article/10448/

95] See http://www.etims.net/index.php?option=com_content&task=view&id=3405&Itemid=2

96] See http://news.bbc.co.uk/democracylive/hi/scotland/newsid_9581000/9581000.stm"http://news.bbc.co.uk/democracylive/hi/scotland/newsid_9581000/9581000.stm

97] Listen to the debate at http://www.battleofideas.org.uk/index.php/2011/session_detail/5736"http://www.battleofideas.org.uk/index.php/2011/session_detail/5736

98] See http://www.bbc.co.uk/sport/0/football/15706740

99] See John Kelly discussing these issues on Listen to the debate at http://www.battleofideas.org.uk/index.php/2011/session_detail/5736"http://www.battleofideas.org.uk/index.php/2011/session_detail/5736

100] Malik, K. (2009) *From Fatwa to Jihad: The Rushdie Affair and its Legacy*. London: Atlantic Books. pp. 68.

101] See http://www.spiked-online.com/index.php?/site/reviewofbooks_article/5515/